Today's preacher h
this book, Lane cal
need to achieve if v
highly distracted w
ing to the next level, this book will help.

-Carey Nieuwhof, *Founding Pastor of Connexus Church
and author of Didn't See It Coming*

In 16 years of pastoring, preaching was the one thing I did, which had the most potential for Kingdom impact, took the most time in my week, and yet where I always felt I could improve. This book reads easily, almost like Lane is sitting with you in a coaching session. I'm thankful for this comprehensive tool to help pastors do what we've been called to do.

-Ron Edmondson, *CEO, Leadership Network*

Two things I know for sure is everyone gets better with a coach and nothing grows a church faster than when a preacher gets better. Lane Sebring has combined these two principles in his new book Become A Preaching Ninja. This resource is a must-have for every preacher and communicator. Lane has given us a gift! Get this book. Not only will you enjoy the results, so will those in your church!

- Brian Dodd, *author or Timeless: 10 Enduring Practices of Apex Leaders and founder of BrianDoddOnLeadership.com*

WOW! There is so much packed into Become a Preaching Ninja! The journey starts with the mindset and ends up with incredibly practical tactics. It's like a masterclass is kick-starting your preaching career! I wish they had this book on preaching when I was back in seminary. Pick up a few copies and go through it with your team!

-Rich Birch, *author of Church Growth Flywheel and founder of UnSeminary*

Preparing and preaching a sermon to a diverse congregation every week is an arduous journey. Thankfully, we have leaders like Lane Sebring publishing helpful books like Become a Preaching Ninja so you can continue your growth as a Gospel communicator.

-Justin Trapp, founder of Ministry Pass and Sermonary

Changing the world through compelling communication and preaching requires a never ending pursuit to improve our skills and strategies as preachers. Lane has written a helpful book full of practical tools that you can use immediately to take your communication to the next level, and see lives changed by the Gospel in the process!

-Rodney Arnold, Lead Pastor of OneLife Church Knoxville, TN

Do you want to take your preaching to the next level? Become a Preaching Ninja is the tool you need. Lane has put together a powerful guide for preachers of all experience levels. I have no doubt that if you put into practice what he teaches, your preaching will improve exponentially.

-Brandon Kelley, coauthor of Preaching Sticky Sermons, cofounder of Sticky Sermons Academy and RookiePreacher.com

People leave churches because the preaching doesn't connect with their lives. Lane Sebring understands how important preaching is to the health and direction of a church and he has used his gifting and experience to write Become a Preaching Ninja. For our preaching to be effective we have to see the value in the details. Things like preparation, practice, humor and the ability to tell stories are intentional ways to communicate truth. Not only will your ministry benefit from reading this book but you will also enjoy Lane's grasp of preaching and the clear way he presents it.

-Barry White, Lead Pastor of Park Valley Church, Haymarket, VA

Many preachers want to become better communicators but they don't know how. This book fleshes out the high calling of preaching and gives practical tools for anyone wanting to effectively communicate God's Word. Pay special attention to Lane's sections on humor and storytelling, for these two often forgotten elements separate the good communicators from the transcendent ones!

-Josh Daffern, Lead Pastor of Centreville Baptist Church, Centreville, VA, blogger at JoshDaffern.com & Patheos.com

Black belts in the art of communication are able to not only clearly convey a message and instruction but do so in a manner that is both captivating and inspiring. And when such an expert takes on the role of sensei to guide a group of eager learners, those in the dojo bow out of respect for and confidence in someone who fully understands the rigors associated with the experience. Lane is that sensei, Become a Preaching Ninja is his dojo, and the guidance he provides is done so in his typically easy-to-follow and personable style that is marked by the right blend of clarity, enthusiasm, and urgency. There is no doubt in my mind that this book will be a tremendous tool in the hands of those committed to maximizing how effectively they teach/preach the most important message that exists.

-John M. Armstrong, author of A Thought-out Faith: Christianity as the Best Explanation and founder of Invictus Maneo Press

Lane Sebring understands that good preaching requires attention to the details. In Become a Preaching Ninja, Lane addresses nearly every element that will impact your effectiveness as a preacher. The principles in this book are incredibly helpful and easy to start implementing right now. Improving in this area can feel challenging and daunting, but Becoming a Preaching Ninja provides a clear roadmap that makes improvement feel doable and enjoyable!

-Tim Coressel, Student and Young Adult Pastor of Cornerstone Church, Boulder, CO

It is a wonderful privilege to preach the Word of God so people can know the God of the Word! It is also an awesome responsibility. A responsibility that begins with focusing on an accurate understanding of the content of the scripture passage being preached. However, those life-changing truths about God and His plan and purpose must be communicated so that people will listen, can understand, and want to apply those truths. Lane Sebring's book, Become a Preaching Ninja, is an excellent resource for both the novice and seasoned preacher to hone their preaching skills and become a better communicator of God's inerrant, authoritative truth. Read, apply, improve – all to the glory of God!

-Dr. Billy F. Ross, Vice-President, Mobilization and Ministry Partnership of World Hope Ministries International

Don't hesitate to read whatever Lane writes. His heart is to help others share God's Word in the most effective and compelling way possible. That's what he writes, and that's what he does. The day I stop learning is the day I should stop teaching. Lane helps me keep learning.

-Elaine Bonds, teacher and speaker M.A.B.S, Dallas Theological Seminary

BECOME A PREACHING NINJA

Sharpen Your Skills, Hone Your Craft, Maximize Your Impact as a Preacher

LANE SEBRING

BECOME A PREACHING NINJA

Published by Preaching Donkey
Knoxville, TN 37912

All rights reserved. No part of this publication may be reproduced, distributed, or transmitted in any form or by any means, including photocopying, recording, or other electronic or mechanical methods, without the prior written permission of the publisher, except in the case of brief quotations embodied in critical reviews and certain other noncommercial uses permitted by copyright law.

Any Internet addresses (websites, blogs, etc.), telephone numbers, authors, and thought-leaders referenced in this book are offered as a resource to the reader. They are not intended in any way to be or imply an endorsement on the part of the author or publisher, nor do they vouch for their content.

Scripture quotations are from the ESV® Bible (*The Holy Bible, English Standard Version*®), copyright © 2001 by Crossway, a publishing ministry of Good News Publishers. Used by permission. All rights reserved. *Italics* in Scripture quotations are the author's emphasis.

Scripture quotations marked (NIV) are taken from the Holy Bible, New International Version®, NIV®. Copyright © 1973, 1978, 1984, 2011 by Biblica, Inc.™ Used by permission of Zondervan. All rights reserved worldwide. www.zondervan.com The "NIV" and "New International Version" are trademarks registered in the United States Patent and Trademark Office by Biblica, Inc.™

Names and events in this book are the product of the author's imagination, based on his years of experience preaching and leading in local church settings and helping others do the same. Any resemblance to any person, living or dead, is coincidental.

Copyright © 2019 Lane Sebring
ISBN-13: 9781727202472
ISBN-10: 1727202473

Printed in the United States of America
First Edition 2019

To the Preaching Donkey community:
Together we strive to preach with more impact and effectiveness than ever before.

CONTENTS

INTRODUCTION

The Danger of Settling for Mediocre Preaching   1

PART ONE: MASTER THE ESSENTIALS

1 Mindset Meltdown   13
Destructive Mindsets That Can Wreck Your Preaching

2 So You Think You Can Preach?   23
Finding Opportunities to Preach

3 Preparation Essentials   33
A Simplified Process for Writing a Sermon

4 Finishing Touches   45
Getting Your Sermon Ready to Preach

5 Preach What You Practice   61
Why Rehearsing Is Essential to Great Sermon Delivery

PART TWO: MASTER THE SECRET WEAPONS

6 Once Upon a Time   77
How Storytelling Changes Everything

7 It Matters How You Tell It   89
The Nitty Gritty of Storytelling

8 That Was Hilarious!   107
Why Humor Is Worth Mastering

9 More Than Joke-Telling 117
How to Use Humor in Your Sermons

PART THREE: MASTER THE EXECUTION

10 The Moment Matters 131
Bringing Your Listeners into an Experience

11 Smooth Delivery 147
Eliminate Distractions, Be Ready for Anything

12 What Are You Talking About? 161
Avoiding the Curse of Knowledge

13 Maximize Engagement 173
Ditch the Notes, Own the Room

CONCLUSION

The One Thing You Can't Do Without 183

ABOUT THE AUTHOR 191

ACKNOWLEDGMENTS

This project is the culmination of many people pouring into me and cheering me on:

Rachel, you have supported me every step of the way and I am exceedingly more grateful for you every day. Thanks for making the sacrifices necessary to let me write this book and share my passion with the world.

Rodney Arnold, I've learned more about preaching from you than anyone I've ever been around. It never ceases to amaze me how you can stand in front of a group of people and captivate, motivate and inspire them to action.

OneLife Church, being on mission with you where we live, work and play is the most fulfilling thing in the world! I can't wait to see God do something so big only He can get the credit!

Preaching Donkey community, you inspire me with your relentless pursuit of excellence in preaching. Always eager to learn, grow and become the kind of communicators God calls you to become. You are my heroes!

Friends, you know who you are. The calls, the texts, the support and the confidence I have that you want to see me win. Thank you. Means more than you know.

God, you have called and equipped me to do your work. This book is the result of an imperfect person making an imperfect attempt to help imperfect people proclaim the truths of a perfect God. I am grateful you let me do this!

INTRODUCTION

The Danger of Settling for Mediocre Preaching

"I would like you to preach at our Sunday night service in a couple weeks. Would you be willing to do that?"

My pastor put this question to me when I was 17 years old. I had just spent my sophomore and junior years of high school wrestling off and on with a feeling I couldn't shake: God is calling me to ministry.

To be honest, during those two years I didn't want to pursue a life of vocational ministry. For various reasons and fears, I was reluctant to be obedient to what I increasingly knew was God's calling on my life. I would fight the urge I felt to relent and obey. Though I didn't realize it at the time, I was fighting the one thing that gives me more joy than anything else I endeavor to do.

But the summer before my senior year in high school things changed for me. Through a lot of soul-searching and contemplating my future I had to face this question: Am I going to be obedient to God even when he's asking me to do something I'm afraid of and don't know if I want?

At the point of my deepest wrestling with my calling, a good friend spoke into my life with a simple question: "Lane, are you running from a call to ministry?" It was as if those words pierced my soul and arrested my unsettled heart. At that point I couldn't fight any more. That summer night in June I said, "God, if you'll still use me, I'm willing to be used."

I'm thankful that God was patient with me and increasingly showed me that the plans he had for me were exactly what was best for me. He designed me and knows me better than I know myself. Armed with nothing more than a sense of calling and a newfound passion for pursuing what God had for me in that calling, I responded to my pastor's invitation to preach with a resounding "Yes!"

I was scared to death and obsessed over every word and every part of that message. I knew right away that this preaching thing was going to require everything I had to give it. I nervously paced back and forth across the stage aimlessly. I raced through the sermon reading nearly every word of it verbatim from my notes. Despite my shaky start, that sermon led to another and another. Soon, I was on staff at a church working in student ministry leading Bible studies, giving messages, and teaching in some capacity multiple times a week.

As a youth pastor for six years, preaching was something I did every single week as the leader of a small church of 150 people – a "church" in the sense that this student ministry was comprised of worship services, small groups, missions, outreach, and all the entertainment a group of teenagers could ask for. But speaking was only one small part of all I did. I felt a pressure to minimize the time and energy I spent preparing messages because I felt a certain guilt attached to it. In fact, I enjoyed it so much that I thought it must not count as "work." I also felt that running the *machine* was what everyone else wanted me to do. Consequently, I did not spend a whole lot of time preparing myself to be better at preaching.

Later when I led a young adult ministry and preached every week in our main worship services, I felt this same pressure not to focus too much on preaching. Preaching was important. I knew that as much as anyone. But I still felt I needed to be doing other things besides working on my messages and on my ability to communicate them effectively.

I have a feeling you have experienced this same pressure. In the leadership-heavy culture most of us pastors find ourselves in, the emphasis is on leading organizations, staffing, fund-raising, building systems, providing pastoral care, connecting people in small groups, equipping volunteers, leading culture, and moving the mission forward. These are all things that have a tremendous importance. But preaching often seems like it takes a backseat in the catalogue of tasks and endeavors we should spend time and effort on as pastors.

PREACHING RARELY GETS THE ATTENTION IT TAKES TO MASTER

Unfortunately, this de-emphasis on preaching as primary has quite a negative result over time. Leaders get better and systems get more streamlined – this is good! But as those aspects of leadership get stronger, the ability to cast a compelling vision that gets everyone on board with the mission lags behind.

When we don't flex our preaching muscle we don't continue to sharpen our preaching skills. We are not continually honing our craft and ultimately maximizing our preaching impact. Instead, we rely on the preaching principles we learned years ago. We would never neglect our leadership like this, but when it comes to preaching, we often don't feel like we have a choice but to neglect it and forego improving our preaching skills in this way. Again, doing this has many serious negative consequences.

Studies show that preaching, including sermon content and the preacher and his preaching skills, is among the top reasons people choose to come back to a church for a second visit or not come back at all. A recent Gallop.com poll shows that "sermon content is what appeals most to churchgoers" with the sermon accounting for 75-76% of the reason cited for coming (or not coming) back for a second visit.[1]

Thom Rainer's group conducted a study to determine the top reasons unchurched people attend a church, and 90% of respondents indicated that the preacher/preaching is the reason they would attend and return (or not return) to a church.[2]

INVEST IN YOUR PREACHING

Given the fact that the quality of preaching accounts for 75-90% of the reasons people give for attending or returning to a church, there is too much at stake for you to neglect investing in your development as a preacher. You have too much to give and too much to lose not to discover how to maximize your preaching impact.

---

[1] https://news.gallup.com/poll/208529/sermon-content-appeals-churchgoers.aspx
[2] https://www.evangelismcoach.org/top-reasons-unchurched-people-choose-a-church/

I'm here to give you permission to invest in your preaching. To invest in yourself. You are going to no longer feel *any* guilt attached to trying to make yourself a better preacher. You are set free from trying to copy someone else's preaching, and you are commissioned to be the preacher that God has designed and called *you* to be. Here's what I believe about you: You *can* make a big impact and you *should* make a bigger impact. This book will help you do that.

ON BECOMING A PREACHING NINJA

According to Dictionary.com, the word *ninja* has two primary definitions:

1. "A member of a feudal Japanese society of mercenary agents, highly trained in martial arts and stealth, who were hired for covert purposes ranging from espionage to sabotage and assassination.
2. "A person who is expert or highly skilled in a specified field or activity (often used attributively)."[3]

The second definition is the one I want to focus on for the purposes of becoming a preaching ninja. But before I do, I think it's important to take a look at the first

---

[3] https://www.dictionary.com/browse/ninja

definition as it explains the essence of ninjutsu — the term used for the art as practiced. Ninjas are highly trained martial artists. Their tactics are stealth and covert. This means that much of the technique a ninja uses is undetectable to the layperson. Ninjas are experts at accomplishing their missions in ways that would look easy to an untrained person but in fact requires years of dedicated practice.

Now, let's look at the second definition. "Ninjas" are experts in their field. They are highly skilled in a given activity. Much like the first definition, ninjas make what they do look easy even though it is not. What they do demands a relentless pursuit to master their craft.

I think you can see where I'm going with this. As preachers, we must master our craft as well. We must become expert and highly skilled at creating and delivering messages that captivate and inspire our audiences.

A preaching ninja is able to deliver a message with clarity and ease of expert execution. But the vast majority of how the preacher has trained and what the preacher has learned and honed through years of training is undetectable to the audience member.

The listener is merely left to grapple with the truth delivered. The preaching ninja is happy to let all those years of training result in what the audience views as seemingly effortless life-changing messages.

To become a preaching ninja requires the same level of dedication and devotion to the craft as mercenary agents hired for assassination would deliver. The good news is we are delivering messages of life-change and not life-end (i.e., assassinations). The only assassination we need to fear is boring everyone to death!

I want you to become a preaching ninja. I want you to sharpen your skills, hone your craft, and maximize your impact as a preacher. I want this for you because I know it's possible, and I know what's at stake if you do not.

So as we charge ahead in this book and dive into principles and practices that you will master as we go, keep in mind that the end-goal is not to be a preaching ninja so you can be satisfied with your hard work. Rather, the end-goal is to preach in such a way that people are moved and lives are changed by the gospel. Becoming a preaching ninja is a necessary first step to that end.

WHAT YOU WILL GET OUT OF THIS BOOK

This book contains three parts that build on one another. The goal of this book is to help you master preaching. But here's something I must tell you: Preaching cannot be *fully* mastered. There is no point any of us reach where we can throw our hands up and say, "I've arrived. I've fully mastered preaching. I have no more room to grow."

Preaching, like any other great art, is inexhaustible. You never reach a point where there is nothing more to improve upon. But, instead of being discouraging, this should thrill you! It excites me because it tells me that I can always make a bigger impact with my preaching. I can always sharpen more skills, hone more of my craft, and continue to maximize my impact as a preacher. Then, I can do it all over again. And again. For the rest of my life.

I want to set you on a journey toward doing just that. Will you "master" preaching? Not fully, but you will be well on your way toward maximizing every ounce of preaching potential God has placed in you. I am thrilled to help you do that.

Part one of this book focuses on mastering the essentials. If you don't have a firm grasp on the fundamentals of preaching, then it will be impossible to move on to the more advanced techniques and skills. In these chapters I will walk you through best practices for your mindset, sermon writing, sermon preparation, and rehearsing your messages before you deliver them.

In part two we will focus on two secret weapons every preacher should master: storytelling and humor. I'm particularly excited about your reading this section because I'm convinced that a firm grasp on masterful storytelling and the ability to use humor well makes all the difference in your ability to capture and maintain interest in your content and consequently make a bigger impact.

Finally, part three drills down on best-practices for mastering the execution – the delivery – of your messages. This section will walk you through how to create powerful moments when you preach and then move your listeners from those moments to movement in their lives. It will also reveal how to eliminate distractions and keep your sermons flowing smoothly. You will discover how to preach without notes and avoid the curse of knowledge which plagues many preachers. This section is all about helping you hone the craft of sermon delivery so that you're presenting at your fullest capacity every time you preach.

For the sake of consistency, this book focuses primarily on preaching in a local church context, but you can apply the principles more broadly to speaking and preaching in any context or environment. I've tried to make the principles as transferable as possible so that you can take them with you any time you get speaking opportunities.

With that foundation laid, let's dive into part one and discover how to master the essentials of preaching!

PART ONE

MASTER THE ESSENTIALS

CHAPTER ONE

Mindset Meltdown
Destructive Mindsets That Can Wreck Your Preaching

You are why I wrote this book. More specifically, your becoming the absolute best preacher possible and making a massive impact for Christ is why I wrote this book. My top priority as I write is to take you on a journey of sharpening your skills, honing your craft, and maximizing your impact as a preacher. Think of this book as a conversation between you and me as if we were discussing preaching over a cup of coffee. As we walk through these chapters together I am not positioning myself as an expert with nuggets of wisdom from on high. Rather, I'm a student of preaching with a passion to help preachers like you make a bigger impact.

I have tried to be open and honest about the areas of my preaching that still need work. And this only works if you do the same as you read. Be willing to be honest with yourself about the places in your preaching that need improvement and development. I am honored to be your guide through this journey. In the chapters that follow you will find actionable best-practices and strategies to master your preaching game. But for now, I want to deal with an important issue that has more to do with how you *think* about preaching than how you actually preach.

One thing I know for sure is that if you have a bad preaching mindset you will not become the kind of preacher God has called you to become. You will not fulfill your greatest preaching potential. A ninja cannot be distracted by thought patterns that run contrary to executing his mission. If we are going to become preaching ninjas – expert and highly skilled in our craft – then we have to develop healthy mindsets and demolish negative ones.

What do I mean by "preaching mindset"? A preaching mindset is the story we tell ourselves about our preaching. It is a narrative, an internal dialogue that no one else can hear and we want to keep it that way! We know that if people could catch a glimpse into our mindset they may rethink both their decision to listen to our preaching and their decision to regard us as a spiritual leader in their lives. But we must deal with destructive mindsets because, try as we may to hide them, their effects become evident in our preaching. And they become evident more and more as we continue to preach through the years.

MINDSETS THAT CAN WRECK YOUR PREACHING

I want to share with you some of the more common destructive preaching mindsets that I have seen wreck people's preaching. In fact, I will speak to my own experience with a few of these because I've been guilty of telling these stories to myself. As you read, you may see yourself in these as well. Here are the four mindsets that we must discover how to overcome.

"I don't need to improve; I know all there is to know about preaching." This mindset is particularly destructive because preachers who think this way generally have a host of blind spots in their preaching and leadership. They think they've got it all covered and don't need to get better, but in most cases the opposite is true.

If this is you it may be because you truly think you have heard everything there is to hear about preaching. You've been exposed to every book, every course, and every tip and trick. While you have certainly heard a lot, you haven't really heard everything, and it doesn't mean that everything you have heard has sunk in and changed you for the better.

Preaching is an endeavor that only works if you remain hungry. You can't lose your hunger to improve and develop your craft. The good news is that if you picked up this book it likely means you are hungry to sharpen your skills and maximize your impact as a preacher. If you begin to apply principles and practices you have heard before I would consider that a win. If you discover some new preaching principles and how-to's you've never thought of before and apply those I would consider that a huge win.

"I don't need to prepare; I'm a natural." One of the most egregious attitudes I see among some preachers is the thought that they can "just wing it" on Sunday. It usually sounds like this: "I'm just better on my feet so I don't need to prepare." Or perhaps, "I know some preachers spend time and energy preparing, but I just get up there and it all comes together." Or sometimes it's spiritualized: "I don't really have to study because the Holy Spirit just leads me in the moment."

Sadly, these statements often stem from arrogance and laziness. I don't mean to sound harsh, but it's true that arrogance is all over a preacher's thinking he is the one person who can pull a powerful, life-changing sermon out of the air in the moment. Instead, what he often pulls out is a sermon that comes across as scattered and without a purposeful aim. Listeners pick up on this and check out because they realize their time is being a wasted by a preacher who didn't respect their limited attention and valuable time enough to prepare.

Laziness comes in because the preacher really just doesn't want to put in the necessary work to prepare something worthy of the attention of an increasingly uninterested, bored, and disengaged audience. This is also a huge blind spot because those who do this often don't understand that the stakes are *way too high* to risk giving an aimless presentation because they did not put in adequate preparation.

In the chapters that follow, I will show you how to prepare not just the sermon but to prepare yourself to make the greatest impact you can make as a preacher. You'll discover that every sermon provides a unique opportunity to develop and sharpen your preaching skills. Every sermon is a blank canvas to which you can apply certain guidelines to make it come together in a powerful way. But to do this you cannot – *cannot* – disregard preparing as beneath you or as an unnecessary use of time and energy.

"I'm a terrible preacher; these people deserve better." Another mindset that can wreak havoc on your preaching in a different way is the thought that you are terrible as a preacher. The problem with this mindset is that it tends to become a self-fulfilling prophecy. This is my relationship with basketball. I feel terrible at basketball, so every time I get on the court to play I'm terrible. I'm not good be-

cause the whole time all I can think is, "I'm so bad at this it's embarrassing. I'm sure these guys are mad they picked me to be on their team." If this is my mindset, there is almost zero chance I'll play well. But the times I go on the court and think, "It's okay, I'll do my best and not stress about it" I tend to play much better.

I think the same is true for preaching. We can all improve and should improve. But when you stand up on Sunday your mindset needs to be, "I'm going to give this all I've got and let God do what only he can do." I hope that by reading this book you'll not only change your mindset but see consistent improvement in your preaching. This will improve your confidence – or better yet, your Godfidence – in what God can do in and through you as a preacher.

"God can't use me in this way – I don't measure up!" Every preacher has felt this way from time to time. And some may feel this way all the time. The aching feeling of not being good enough to preach is common among preachers. It takes on different forms, but preachers often feel a pressure to appear more spiritual than they really are. This pressure leads them to perform in a sense and try to come across as more spiritual than they actually experience. This leads to a sense of guilt and the feeling of being an imposter. Imposter syndrome, the feeling that you fall way short of the expectations that come with your role, is common among preachers.

This mindset is exacerbated by the particular tradition you find yourself in. Pastors in more moralistic traditions may feel like their lives don't live up to the strict standards they've set for others. Preachers in more charismatic and Pentecostal settings may feel deep down that they lack the gifts and abundant faith they call others to display. Those in a more Reformed tradition may feel a sense of intellectual inadequacy because they know the theological muscles they are expected to have and to flex. Whatever the case, any preacher in any tradition can feel just not good enough. This feeling can seem humble and even spiritual at times. For some it can become the "what a worm I am" mindset that comes across as self-deprecating in a *holy* way.

The danger of this mindset is that it takes the power and emphasis off God and puts it on ourselves as the arbiters of effectiveness. We think that unless we start to measure up, God will not be able to use our preaching to his ends and for his glory. You cannot maximize your preaching impact with this way of thinking.

A SHIFT NEEDS TO HAPPEN

There are countless destructive mindsets that we as preachers can adopt that will wreck our preaching. Identify any unhelpful or destructive mindset(s) you may have about your preaching. You may resonate with one of the four mentioned above or a variety of other potentially destructive mindsets. Maybe you compare yourself to other preachers you admire and feel as if your talents and gifting are lacking. Perhaps you have such anxiety around preaching that the thought of your next sermon makes you feel nauseated. Or maybe you don't know where to start when you go to prepare and it just overwhelms you to the point of wanting to give up on preaching altogether.

Whatever the case, you have to shift your mindset from doubting your abilities to trusting in God's ability to do something amazing and life-changing through your preaching. If no one has ever told you this before, let me be the first: Although you may not think God can change the world through your words, he can, and I want to help you do your part. I believe that if you are called by God and surrendered to him he can take your words and change the world with them.

I want to be your guide. I want to walk you through a process of becoming the best preacher you can possibly be. It starts with changing the way you think. It starts with moving from a destructive mindset that places too much confidence in your own abilities and not enough in God's. If you're on the other side it starts with choosing to understand that God changes lives, not you. Therefore your confidence is fully in God. You want to bring the best you have every time and leave the results up to God.

It starts with shifting your ideas about what God can accomplish through your preaching.

A MINDSET SHIFT IS NOT ENOUGH

Shifting your mindset to rid yourself of destructive ways of thinking about your preaching is important and vital. But a mindset shift alone is not enough. The renewed mindset must be coupled with new preaching practices. You have to adopt new principles that change your habits and the way you prepare and deliver sermons.

This book is intended to help you with both. You will discover a new way of thinking about each sermon you prepare. You'll develop confidence in your abilities knowing that you are bringing your best and God is doing the rest. You will also discover tools to help you with the most nitty gritty, practical elements of great sermon preparation and delivery.

You'll dive deep into storytelling and using humor in your messages. You'll discover how to improve the quality of how you deliver your message by ditching the notes and avoiding common presentation mistakes that detract and distract from your message. You will nail down how to speak to a variety of different people in various spiritual conditions. You will learn how to present complicated truths in ways that new believers and those who are merely curious about spiritual things can understand and apply.

In other words, you will change. Your preaching will change. Your approach to preparing and delivering a sermon will look different. When you couple the change in your mindset with the new preaching principles you are going to learn to apply, your preaching will be next-level and unstoppable. I can't wait to see you in action.

In the next chapter we will dive into laying the foundation for getting started preaching. If you are already established in your role you may want to skip chapter two and move on to chapter three. But, keep in mind that if you know any aspiring preachers, the next chapter will help them get started in their preaching journey.

CHAPTER TWO

So You Think You Can Preach?
Finding Opportunities to Preach

You sit in church and look up at your pastor giving the message and daydream about what it would be like to be the one giving the message.

You get cut off in traffic, lose it for a second, and start pounding your horn. When you calm down it hits you: This would make a great self-deprecating sermon illustration I could use to demonstrate that, while I'm still human, God uses imperfect people.

When someone asks you a question about the Bible, God, theology, a doctrinal dispute, or a social issue, you relish the opportunity to help them make sense of the question, but what you really want is for them to do something with their newly discovered truth.

If any or all of these resonate with you it may mean you have an itch, a desire, perhaps even a calling to preach. I want to share with you some possible next steps you could take to get started preaching. But first, let's answer an important question.

WHO SHOULD PURSUE PREACHING?

Should anyone pursue preaching? The obvious, but most important, question is: Do you have a relationship with Jesus? Are you a follower of Christ? If you are not, then you should not preach. At least not in a Christian context. I can't speak for other faiths, but I would imagine this would be true in almost any religious system: *If you don't believe it yourself, you should not teach or preach it to others.*

Beyond that baseline it is important to make sure that you are growing in your faith and experiencing life with Jesus. Are you pursuing Jesus? Are you readily confessing sin? Are you seeking to multiply your faith to others by sharing your story and helping others discover Jesus? Is there a reason why people would not see you as trustworthy or as a person of character? This is not to say you need to be perfect. No pastor or preacher is perfect. But this *is* to say that your effectiveness as a preacher will be damaged if there are character issues in your life that you have not dealt with. Keep in mind, I am not speaking of your past. Rather, I am asking: Where are you with Jesus at this point in your life, and have others had an opportunity to see the change he has made in you?

Paul gives his requirements for those seeking the position or office of elder (overseer, pastor) in 1 Timothy and Titus. Keep in mind that those requirements are for the position itself. So if a pastoral position is something you seek you should take a look at his requirements and see how your life stacks up. Incidentally, this good for any follower of Christ to do from time to time. Take a look at what is required of those who lead and ask yourself: Am I walking with God in such a way that I could lead others in an official capacity?

It is important to understand the difference between the role of pastor and the function of a pastor. A lot of times these are one and the same, but there are laypersons who have a desire and are gifted at preaching who may be called on to fill in for their pastor. Or you may be in high school or college and trying to determine God's calling on your life. You may be in the corporate world but have developed a strong desire to preach and teach. What do you do with that? This chapter will help you sort through those questions and determine how God might be leading you.

In any case, if you are following Jesus and have dealt with any known sin issues in your life, and you have a desire to pursue preaching, you should do that. You're not going to be perfect. I know I'm not. Neither is your pastor. Follow Jesus closely and live a Spirit-filled life, and you will be ready to go.

STEPS TO GET STARTED PREACHING

Now that you have the foundation for *who* should pursue preaching, where do you go from here? You have a desire to preach, but you don't know where to begin. I want to give you a step-by-step process to get you started preaching no matter your beginning point.

Start where you are. Maybe you envision yourself as the next Craig Groeschel, Andy Stanley, Matt Chandler, or Steven Furtick. It's fine to have some preaching heroes and draw inspiration from your favorite pastors. But you have to begin where you are. If you've never preached or taught in front of a group of people, you are probably not going to be called on to give the Sunday sermon next week at your church. So you need to begin within your context.

I knew I was called to ministry at age 15 and strongly fought that feeling for two years. I had a lot of doubts and fears about whether God could use me in that way, and if I even wanted that for my life. If you've ever been called to do something you didn't initially want to do you will be able to relate. But, at 17 years of age I said, "God, if you'll still use me, I'm willing." As a senior in high school I didn't have the opportunity to preach the Sunday morning sermon, at least not yet. But what I did do was team up with another friend and we led a Bible study for sophomore guys. I taught every other Monday night and loved it. I honed my skills and was able to seek more opportunities from there.

So hang on to your aspirations and goals, but look around and start right where you are. Identify those in your circle with whom you have influence and can speak into their lives. Be willing to mentor or coach one or two people, and God will open up opportunities to speak to more people. This leads to the next step.

Seek out opportunities. If you have a desire to preach look for any opportunity that is in front of you: Are you in a Bible study, small group, or Sunday school class? The leader may gladly give you the opportunity to teach or lead a week. Though teaching and preaching are very similar, there is a difference between the two. It will help to learn both skills.

Is there a nursing home or jail in your area that has a regular church service? Find out who leads it and see if they would like a fill-in. Ask your pastor what opportunities are available. Perhaps your pastor will be willing to coach you and get you ready to preach a sermon at your church. This is especially possible if your church has a midweek service or a Sunday night service that is different from Sunday morning. There are usually fewer people in attendance and a more laid-back atmosphere at such evening services. Your pastor may be more than willing to take a night off and let you do what you're itching to do.

What speaking and preaching opportunities are there in your student and children's ministries? You can learn a ton about communication when speaking to kids. If you're not crystal clear, concise, and compelling, kids will not listen. In fact, from a teaching perspective, if you can explain a concept in a way that a child would understand it, you can explain it to anyone.

When seeking out opportunities, you should keep two things in mind: First, It never hurts to ask. If you want an opportunity, ask for it. Your pastor may not think you're ready, and you should not take this personally. Instead, ask what you can do to get better and then communicate with your actions that you are serious about pursuing preaching. Most pastors relish the opportunity to coach an aspiring communicator, but they don't want to waste their time on someone who is not taking it seriously.

Second, be willing to take every chance you get. If you're serious about growing as a new preacher, you will not pass up any opportunity. Look at each preaching assignment as a way to discover and develop your calling. No opportunity is too small.

Ask for meaningful feedback. Every time you present content to people you should seek meaningful feedback.

People will be tempted to tell you that you did an amazing job because they won't want to crush your spirits as a new preacher. That type of encouragement is fine and you'll get a good amount of it. But you need to seek out honest feedback from people who will give you specific critiques so you will know what to work on for the next time. No one is an expert at something right out of the gate. The best athletes in the world spend countless hours conditioning and practicing. Preaching is much the same – it take hours of effective practice to become proficient. It takes countless more to master it. Be willing to receive feedback from trusted people and make adjustments accordingly.

Confirm your calling. You will seek opportunities to preach and you will take them. You'll teach, lead Bible studies, preach, and lead people. These will either be the most energizing, life-giving, soul-enriching experiences of your life or you will hate every second of them.

You'll seek honest feedback from others. The majority of what you'll hear will be, "You've got a gift, God has equipped you to do this, continue to hone this skill, and it will be amazing to see what God will do in and through you." Or you won't hear much of anything. Deep down inside you will feel a desire to do more of it, or you won't. What I'm trying to say is that the idea of "calling" is not all that mystical.

God confirms calling in a variety of ways. The best way to find out is to do it and see where it leads. If it leads to more and more opportunities that are fulfilling, then it may be a calling. If it leads to dread and drudgery for you and your listeners, it may not be a calling.

Keep in mind as well that a calling to preach does not always mean a calling to be a lead pastor or staff pastor at a church. It could mean that you preach and teach as a layperson when asked or you have an itinerant ministry where you travel and preach or serve in a nursing home or prison ministry. A calling to preach could have a host of different applications for different people. The point is: Seek God's direction, pray for him to lead you, and see what fulfills you and leaves you itching for more.

Avail yourself of preaching resources. There are a plethora of books, blogs, podcasts, and other helpful preaching aids online. I want to share with you some resources we've provided at Preaching Donkey to help you get started. Check out our list of *The Best 5 Books on Preaching,* which you can find on our website at PreachingDonkey.com. Listen to *The Preaching Donkey Podcast,* which is available on most podcast providers. Make sure you're subscribed to the email list at Preaching Donkey, which will keep you up-to-date with the latest preaching resources we've provided. Finally, check out my first book, *Preaching Killer Sermons: How to Create and Deliver Messages that Captivate and Inspire,* which will give you more tools to apply as you hone your skill as a preacher. I will refer to that book regularly in the chapters that follow as that book and this one work hand in hand to help you prepare and deliver sermons at your best.

Consider formal training. Finally, you may want to consider formal training such as seminary. Though this is not necessary in every context, it could be helpful if you are looking to pursue an official position as a lead pastor or teaching pastor. Though my bachelor's degree is in Communication from a state university, I do have a master's degree from a seminary. There's nothing magical about having a seminary degree, but it did expose me to concepts that have helped me as a pastor and preacher. The pastoral role has particular challenges and requires certain skills often not addressed in seminary. But seminary is helpful for preaching because it teaches you how to handle the Bible appropriately when studying and teaching it.

As part of your training, consider pursuing internships. If you are just beginning in ministry I would highly suggest doing an internship at the kind of church you envision yourself leading. I was able to complete two long-term internships at a couple of great churches when I was completing my bachelor's degree. That experience set me up for success and prepared me to take a full-time role at my first church.

Those are the best first steps to getting started preaching. I know that many of you reading this book are already well on your journey of preaching, but consider new or aspiring preachers you could share this information with to help them get started.

For those getting started preaching, imagine that you've led some Bible studies and small groups and you're feeling relatively confident about teaching in small group contexts. But recently your pastor has tapped you on the shoulder and said, "Would you preach on Sunday night in two weeks?" Or you got a call from a church that is without a pastor asking you to fill in next Sunday.

This is so exciting! This is what you've been waiting for! But you have some aching questions: What do I do? Where do I start? A sermon is different from what you've done to this point. A lesson in a small group can go a lot of different ways. There is interaction and dialogue. In most cases, a sermon relies on you to carry the content from start to finish. This thought both terrifies and exhilarates you. By the way, the emotions of terror and exhilaration are part of what make preaching so fun and interesting. Embrace those feelings and keep moving forward.

CHAPTER THREE

Preparation Essentials
A Simplified Process for Writing a Sermon

If I'm being honest, sermons are fun to deliver, but not so much fun to write. Writing a sermon can be a vexing task for many preachers. In fact, the question I get the most from the thousands of preachers who subscribe to PreachingDonkey.com is some version of: "How can I get more efficient at writing my sermons?" Or "Sermon prep is my biggest struggle; what advice do you have to make it faster and easier?" Most pastors are busy, and it is nearly impossible to free up hours of dedicated time for study.

There's good news and bad news. The bad news is there is no substitute for thorough sermon preparation.

The better you prepare, the better the sermon. And good sermon preparation takes time. But, the good news is that you can make better use of sermon prep time if you have an efficient plan and well-thought-out steps. The process of writing a sermon can be daunting and tedious. This is why a system of steps will help you simplify the process and know exactly what you've accomplished and what still needs to be done for every sermon you write.

I have developed a step-by-step system to take your sermon from conception to delivery. If you work through action steps, you'll have a sermon written and be ready to go. Additionally, the more sermons you write using this method, the easier and more efficient it will become. The steps will begin to be natural and second nature to you as you begin to conceptualize and write a sermon or develop a series of sermons.

Before I show you the steps required to write a sermon, I want to give you one overarching principle to keep in mind.

CONTENT IS KING

The most important principle to keep in mind when writing sermons is: Content is king. A lot of preachers, but especially new preachers tend to want to look and sound impressive in their delivery. They want people to walk away saying, "Wow! What a natural!" This desire is not necessarily bad. You certainly don't want people walking away mumbling to themselves, "That was rough."

In my writing at Preaching Donkey and in my first book, *Preaching Killer Sermons*, I have not been shy about my dedication to helping preachers communicate as effectively as possible. I believe strongly in compelling delivery because I want pastors to connect to the hearts, minds, and emotions of their listeners in a powerful way (more on this in part 3 of this book).

But as you write your sermon, make great content development your highest aim. Your sermon content needs to be rock solid. This will work out in your favor later because if you structure your content the way I teach, it will lend itself to effective delivery. But it won't be just because you project your voice in the right way. It will be because the content builds tension, creates interest, shows people how to interact and wrestle with the Scriptures, points people to Jesus, and motivates them to take action on what they've heard. With that foundational principle laid, you are now ready to start developing your sermon. Let's dive into the process.

DETERMINE A TOPIC, TITLE, & HOOK

Every sermon is going to have three structural elements that lay the foundation upon which you'll build the message: topic, title and hook.

Determining the topic. To determine the topic you need to decide what your message will be about. This could be a general theme that's rooted in a particular passage of scripture or message series. Or it could be a specific topic that you'll use various Scriptures to teach. Perhaps you are going to preach on forgiveness, or generosity, or pride, or love, or the gospel. Perhaps your church is working through a series and your message will fit into that series. Or maybe you are working through a book of the Bible and will teach the passage that is next in the book.

Whatever the case, your topic should be relatively easy to determine and should take the least amount of time to figure out. The point is to have one so you can begin building upon it. As we work through these steps together, I will use *worry* as our example topic and walk through the steps using it.

Developing a title. The next step is to develop a tentative title for your message. I use the word tentative because the title will likely change as you dig into your content, but ==having a working title will help give you a direction to keep heading as you write==.

Keep in mind that these steps are progressive and help build on each other. When you have a topic and a working title it continues to solidify the direction you are going to take the sermon. The passage of scripture you study is a crucial part of determining these steps and your study should be done concurrently with them (more on that in the next section).

For our example sermon on worry, I'm going to make the tentative title: *From Worry to Peace*. Notice this title is nothing fancy, and I may change it as I move along in writing the sermon or I may keep it as-is. I chose this as my working title because I'm already thinking about what my hook will be. What is a hook?

Crafting a hook. The hook of your sermon is what initially makes people interested in the content. The hook is what makes them give you their attention and think to themselves, "I need to hear more." If I were to walk up on stage, open my Bible, and say, "Today we're going to talk about worry," I've merely stated a fact. My audience is now informed of what the message is about. It's about worry. Yawn. Most people are asking, "Worry? Yeah, it's a thing. So what? Why is this going to matter to me?" Even if they experience worry on a routine basis they are still going to need more information to be convinced that the message is something to which they should give their limited attention.

Let's contrast that with this simple change: "Today we're going to discover how to ditch worry and experience lasting peace." This is a hook because it has signaled to my listeners that the sermon will add value to their lives and benefit them in some way if they pay attention. Questions arise such as "How can I ditch worry?" and "Is peace really possible for me?" Let me point out that this is not a fancy hook; it is not worded in the most creative way; and that is intentional. It doesn't have to be sophisticated. I want you to see that a simple hook can work *if* presented well.

At this point, try not to get bogged down in making a super creative hook to your message. Rather, in this step simply answer this one question: "*Why* should someone listen to this message?" In this case there is a simple reason: *to ditch worry and experience lasting peace.* It's really that simple.

If you want to look into this more broadly you can read about developing the objective and desired response for your sermons in chapter four of my book *Preaching Killer Sermons*. It provides the 30,000-foot view of what I am describing in more detail here. Now that we have a topic – worry, a working title – "From Worry to Peace," and a hook – "Discover how to ditch worry and experience lasting peace," we are ready for our next step, which is to dig into the scripture.

DIG INTO SCRIPTURE

As I mentioned above, it is good to study the scripture concurrently with all steps in the process but especially as you are developing your topic, title, and hook. Many great volumes have been dedicated to studying scripture for sermon preparation. It is not in the scope of this book to provide an exhaustive method for studying the Scriptures for sermon prep. Rather, I want to give an overview of the system I use to study for a sermon. You can apply this system to any type of sermon whether topical, expository, or both. Whether preaching on a particular topic or through books of the Bible, it's good to anchor your message to a particular passage of Scripture and then pull in other supporting texts as needed to support and bolster your points.

How do you study a passage to preach on it? In *Living by the Book: The Art and Science of Reading the Bible*, Howard Hendricks details a simple three-step process to study any passage of Scripture. These steps are:

- *Observation:* "What do I see?"
- *Interpretation:* "What does it mean?"
- *Application:* "How does it work?"

This simple method of study is a fantastic foundational tool. If you can master the art of this method you will be able to look at any passage of scripture and see the teaching gems in it quickly. Let's take a look at each step a little more closely.

Step One: Observation. What do I see? In this step you simply read the passage and make notes about everything you see. What is it saying? What arguments does it make? Look for connecting words such as *like, and, but, therefore,* and *so that.* These show cause and effect. Look for verbs because they show what's happening. In short, spend a lot of time reading and re-reading the passage as many different ways as you can and write down everything that comes to mind about what you see. It's important to pray through this process and let the Holy Spirit teach you something about the passage before you move to other sources such as commentaries and Bible handbooks.

Step Two: Interpretation. What does it mean? This step takes it to the next level and asks, What is the meaning behind what it says? What truths does it point to? This is when you look for the way it fits into the whole of the Bible. You're looking at context: what comes before it and after it in the Bible. You're looking at the history and culture of the time it was written to get an accurate picture of what it means.

This is when you would begin looking at commentaries and using the helps in a good study Bible. I recommend the *ESV Study Bible* and *IVP Bible Background Commentary for the New Testament* to get you started. You can also check out the *IVP Bible Background Commentary for the the Old Testament* if you're working through an Old Testament passage. But there are a lot of free resources online at websites such as Biblegateway.com and Biblehub.com.

Step Three: Application. How does it work? Lastly, in this step you are looking for how the passage applies to everyday life. The benefit of this process is that if you've completed the two previous study steps you will have a rich understanding of what the passage says and what it means. It will naturally flow that you see all the variety of ways it applies. It is important to consider people in all different spiritual conditions and life-stages and from all different backgrounds and experiences.

Write down everything that comes to mind about how your listeners could be able to apply the scripture. Some questions to consider: Is there an example to follow? Is there a command to obey? Is there a truth to embrace? Is there a next step to take? These questions will help you get application ideas flowing.

I highly recommend grabbing a copy of Howard Hendricks' *Living by the Book* and devouring every page of it. It was recommended to me when I first started preaching and was the best gift I could have received. I'm confident you will benefit from it as well.

Let's take a look at our example sermon on worry. For this sermon I focused on Philippians 4:6-7: "Do not be anxious about anything, but in everything by prayer and supplication with thanksgiving let your requests be made known to God. And the peace of God, which surpasses all understanding, will guard your hearts and your minds in Christ Jesus."

Working through the steps above I studied intently what this passage says, what it means, and how it works. I've discovered, among other things, that there is a command "Do not be anxious," which has an actionable step attached to it: "In prayer, give your concerns to God," which in turn has a corresponding promise: "God's peace will guard your hearts and minds in Christ Jesus." I've determined what it means in context by studying the culture of that time. I've checked with commentaries to make sure my assumptions are not off course.

Finally, I've written down a list of ways people can use this passage in their lives and put it into action by obeying the command and embracing the promise and as a result experience peace. By the end of this exercise this list is going to be quite extensive.

A quick note before we move on to the next step. You will not use everything you discovered in your study, and that is fine! You want to be working from a wealth of knowledge on the topic, not a deficit. If you attempt to preach on a text about which you have only a cursory knowledge you will find yourself stumbling through it trying to solidify your thoughts on it in the moment. This is not good for you or your listeners.

Typically I will use 25-30% of what I studied. Why not 100%? Because the sermon would be three hours long! So why study so much? The more you gain a command of the text and topic the better you'll be able to teach on them with ease. Your biggest problem will be overcoming the curse of knowledge, which we will deal with in chapter twelve.

FURTHER READING

Before we move on to putting the finishing touches on the sermon, I want to recommend some books that will help you with a branch of theology called hermeneutics. Hermeneutics is a fancy word for how we interpret and understand the Bible. One of the best skills you can develop as a preacher is how to properly navigate the text and understand it accurately and in context.

I want to recommend three must-reads to you that will help you develop the skill of interpreting the Bible. First, *According to Plan* by Graeme Goldsworthy is an incredible explanation of biblical theology that shows how the story of the Bible all fits together from start to finish.

Second, *Getting the Message* by Daniel M. Doriani is one of the best books I've read on how to understand and interpret the Bible in its original context. This was one of my absolute favorite assigned books in seminary because it allowed me to see how the Scriptures fit together and tell the story of the gospel so beautifully. In my opinion it's a must-read for any Bible teacher or preacher.

Finally, *Let the Reader Understand* by Dan McCartney and Charles Clayton is a great introductory read for anyone looking to gain a better understanding of how to read and interpret the Scriptures.

Now that we have established a topic, title, and hook and have a tight grasp on how to dig into the scriptures effectively and efficiently, let's move on to put the finishing touches on our sermon in the next chapter.

CHAPTER FOUR

Finishing Touches
Getting Your Sermon Ready to Preach

At this point in your study you have established a topic, a title, and a hook. You have thoroughly studied the primary passage of scripture and other supporting texts. You have taken notes on what you've observed from the passages. As you've taken notes your thoughts have begun to form around what you would want to communicate in a sermon.

Some of the heavy lifting is over because at this point you've done so much foundational work that the sermon structure should come naturally. If it doesn't at first, it certainly will as you do this more. This, like any other endeavor, requires practice to hone your skill and achieve expert level.

BUILD AN OUTLINE

In this step you will put it all together to build an outline. This will be the basic bones of your message. I will break down all the elements of an outline and show you how to put yours together.

Determine your Main Idea. You will decide on a main idea or a bottom line that will anchor your message and satisfy the tension you built with your hook. Remember, the hook is designed to entice interest. Your topic may not entice interest on its own but a solid hook will. The reason a hook entices interest is that it points to a problem and teases a solution.

Going back to our example sermon on worry, our hook was to "discover how to ditch worry and experience lasting peace." The tension this hook begins building is that each person has worries. I will spend time massaging that tension at the beginning of the message. The solution it teases is the idea that there is a way to experience lasting peace. It teases it because it doesn't say how yet. It merely points to the solution implying that the sermon will ultimately guide the listener to solve the problem.

Your main idea states in one phrase how your hook will be applied and answered in your sermon. It is the key idea or payoff, so to speak, for staying engaged. If your listeners stick with you, they will walk away with a solution to their worry problem. It is the "if you don't pay attention to anything else I say, listen to this one thing" anchor that holds your sermon together.

In the example sermon, the main idea could simply be: *To experience lasting peace, give your worries to the Prince of Peace.* This answers the "what" of the sermon. What do I ultimately want people to walk away with? In this case, if nothing else, I want my listeners to know that the way to ditch their worries is not to try harder to overcome them, it's not to put them out of their mind, it's not to think more positively, it is to thrust them on God and allow him to guard their hearts and minds as they rest in Christ. The remainder of the outline supports the main idea and fleshes out "how" to apply it.

Build tension and create interest. Building tension is a concept that Andy Stanley developed for our generation of preaching influencers. Put simply, building tension involves getting your listeners interested in the content before you start teaching it. Building tension could be where you get your listeners to feel a problem before you point toward a resolution to that problem. It makes them wrestle with the question before you offer an answer. Tension building begins with your title and hook. Though you will continue to build tension throughout the message, stoke it especially in the beginning of the message.

I cannot overstate how important this step is to a strong sermon structure. The way you use and build tension, especially toward the beginning of your message, determines how much people are going to be tuned in and interested in your content. A message without tension is like a story without conflict. It happens but nobody cares. If you have ever started reading a book without the tension of conflict, chances are you didn't stick around to The End. Tension is the key to interest and engagement.

How do you build tension? It's actually quite simple. You want to point to a question, problem, rub, conflict, issue, annoyance, struggle, or pain that your audience can relate to. Then, massage that tension by applying it to as many people in as many situations as you can think of. Your goal should be to keep building tension until everyone in the room feels it along with you and has a vested interest in it. You want them to perk up and think, "So what do I do about it?"

In my example sermon on worry, I would touch on a number of ways we worry and a number of things we worry about. My goal here is to get everyone to perk up and say, "I can relate to that" or "Yeah, I worry about that too." I want to give people reasons to keep listening and the way to do that is to build tension.

Resolve the tension with the text. After I have built tension by presenting a problem, question, or struggle that everyone can relate to, I point people to the text for the solution to the problem or answer to the question. Taking people to the text empowers them to know the heart of God, understand the gospel, and live in light of it.

At this point I've studied Philippians 4:6-7 thoroughly and know how I want to walk people through that passage. I'm not going to attempt anything complicated or fancy because the passage is so straightforward. Instead, I will walk my listeners through Paul's arguments and ultimately show how this passage points to the solution to worry. I would walk them through this basic logical flow conversationally using the text as my guide and making points along the way:

- Don't worry about anything. Then what should I do?
- Pray about everything. How?
- Ask God for what you need.
- Beg him for relief from what worries you.
- Be thankful for what he's done. Then what?
- God's inexplicable peace will guard your heart and mind from worry.

When drawing points out of this text, I would massage the wording a bit and see how it looks visually, how it sounds when I say it, and how I can best communicate these ideas in a way that gives people the essence of what Paul is advocating while pointing to the ultimate goal of getting his readers *to experience lasting peace by giving their worries to the Prince of Peace.*

My points could be the three statements below. These serve as both "points" and statements that the listener can personalize and internalize. This helps them relate the truths in the passage to their everyday experience:

1) When I worry it results in panic, but when I pray it results in peace.
2) When I ask God for what I need, I will thank him for what he's done.
3) When I experience God's peace, I will rest in him.

I prefer points that accompany the text in order so that making the points feels like a natural walk through of the text. Each point serves as summary and application statement for that part of the text – all of which support and bolster the main idea. Underlined words would be blanks on their printed handout. Those words would also be highlighted on the screens in the room for emphasis.

Teach and illustrate how to apply it. As I walk people through the text and make points my goal is to teach and illustrate how to apply them. I want each person to wrestle with how the text applies to them personally. Later I will explain how to teach, illustrate and apply every point you make so that your listeners fully understand them and put them into action in their lives.

Cast vision and inspire. Finally, I cast a vision of what it would look like if we all applied the main idea. This involves painting a picture of how different our church would be or how much freer we would feel or how much more of an impact we could make on our community if we all were to be obedient to what God has shown us in his word through this sermon.

In my example sermon I might say something like, "Can you imagine what God could do through a group of people who have truly given their worries to him? Everyone around you is wracked with anxiety and worries. What if you were the one person who had an inexplicable peace? Imagine the impact you could have on those around you. They would be drawn to that."

Then I would go on to cast a vision for being a church filled with people who applied the truth. How much of an impact could we make on our city? What would people say about such a countercultural movement of people solely trusting in God's provision and at perfect peace?

The goal here is to get people to feel a sense of anticipation and excitement about participating in living out this truth together. You don't want to make it drudgery where people are thinking, "Okay, I guess I'll do this so I won't feel guilty." No! You want people saying, "Why wouldn't I do what God says to do!" You want to paint a picture so vivid that people do not want to miss out on what God has for them.

At this point you've established a topic, a title, and a hook for your sermon. You've developed an outline that creates tension and points to the text for a solution and then calls people to action. Your sermon foundation is laid and it is ready to be built out and fleshed out. We'll begin with how to build out your points to get the most out of them.

GETTING THE MOST OUT OF YOUR POINTS

For our example sermon on worry, I listed the points earlier in this chapter. At this point in writing my sermon I would look at each one of them and make sure I am doing three things with them: teaching, illustrating, and applying them.

You make points in every sermon you preach. You try to communicate at least one point. One main idea. One bottom line. You may have one major point but a number of supporting points. The point is, you make points. Get the point? So, what do you do with every point you make? Is it enough just to say the words, "My main point is _____. Okay, let's close in prayer." Well, we all know that would be insufficient.

We have to do more than just state a point for it to stick. But how do we do this? How do we develop sticky points that land on people in powerful ways? I suggest doing at least three things with every point you make in your sermons. Using these as a baseline allows you to do more if you'd like, but make sure you're at least doing these three things:

Teach the point. When you teach the point you are explaining the concept and providing the biblical backing. In other words, you are showing how you derived the principle from the Scriptures as you connect it back to the text. This is an important part of making a point. You want to be able to demonstrate that the point is not just your own musings but comes from scripture.

In this step you teach the concept of the point. In other words, you should answer the question your listeners will have when you introduce an idea: *"What do you mean?"*

If this is murky, let me use an example of a super simple point you could make in your sermon. Let's say your point is: God loves you. You may teach this point by referencing John 3:16 and showing your listeners that God loves them so much that he gave his one and only son so that they could have eternal life by believing in him. Perhaps you elaborate a bit on this idea and dig into the theological and biblical truths of the doctrine of God's love for people.

Teaching the point is great, but if you only teach concepts and ideas you're missing two more important steps that put flesh and blood on your points: illustrating and applying.

Illustrate the point. When you illustrate your point you are answering the question, *"What does this look like?"* You are providing a vivid visual that helps your listeners see it and feel it for themselves. How can you get your listeners to feel the emotions of the truth and not just "know" it? You have to make it come alive with illustration. An illustration could be a story, a metaphor, an analogy, a movie clip, news story, or something trending on social media. It can really be anything that helps you clarify the concept of the point and give people an opportunity to feel the weight of it.

Remember our example point: God loves you. One of the best demonstrations of illustrating this point with a story is actually a set of three parables Jesus told in Luke 15 about the love of God for those who are lost or wayward. Side note: Jesus often used stories, or parables, to illustrate his points. In fact, it is rare in Jesus' teaching to see him merely teach a point without painting a vivid illustration usually in narrative form. So be careful if you think storytelling is a lower form of teaching and the elites and sophisticated preachers stick to exposition alone. If this is your assumption, you're missing a powerful tool Jesus used.

Let's say you decide to focus on the last of the three parables Jesus tells in Luke 15 and you tell the story of the prodigal son. In this story, a son took his inheritance before his father died effectively communicating to him: "You're dead to me!" Then he went to a foreign land, squandered his wealth on hookers and booze, and came crawling back in desperation. There is much to be said about this story. In fact I highly suggest you check out Tim Keller's book *The Prodigal God* as it looks at this story from the perspective of the reckless love of the father and the older brother's legalism.

But for our purposes of illustrating our simple point that God loves you, we will focus on the crux of the narrative. The story hits home when we see the prodigal deciding to come home and hoping to plead with his father for mercy and to be allowed to serve as one of his hired men. Instead, his father ran to him, embraced him, kissed him, and threw a massive party for him. How many of us feel the love of the Father for us when we consider this story? Your listeners will too. This is the power of illustration.

This illustration came straight from the pages of scripture. As I mentioned above, it's also helpful to use illustrations from all different aspects of life. So perhaps you could build on the story of the prodigal son and personalize it to your own experience of when you strayed from God but as a loving father he took you back.

Apply the point. When you apply the point you answer the question, *"How does it work?"* A point in a sermon is just information until it takes on flesh and is lived out. Your listeners need to know how this truth can be activated in their lives. This is also where you take the concept, what you've taught and illustrated, and make it useful and practical.

Revisiting our point one last time: God loves you. You may ask the question, "Do you truly believe God loves you or do you still feel unlovable?" Or "What could you do this week to allow yourself to embrace God's love for you?"

In addition to questions and challenges, application could also simply be your touching on several life situations and circumstances and acknowledging the various ways your listeners struggle with embracing this truth.

Although this usually works best in the order I suggested here, you should avoid approaching this process with a formulaic way of thinking, "First I teach, then I illustrate, then I apply." You, and your listeners, will eventually tire of such a stilted approach. Instead, sometimes you may decide to begin with application before you ever teach the concept. This is a great way to make your listeners care about it because they feel it before they know fully what the concept is.

This is called building tension, and it is a crucial part of effective sermon delivery. You have to make people *feel* before they will be likely to respond. Applying the point by building tension and letting that tension (problem, conflict, question) sit in your listeners' hearts and minds can be an effective way to capture them and allow them to see the importance of being obedient to God and applying what the Scripture is teaching.

Most importantly, when you apply the point you want to give your listeners a specific call to action that allows them to take the next step on their faith journey, whatever that is. It may be different for each person, so you have to think through how best to communicate action steps to people who are listening from different spiritual levels. With enough practice this can become somewhat natural.

Other times you may begin with a story that will serve as an amazing illustration to clarify your point once you teach it. There is more than one way to make a point. Get the point? Here's my point: You want to do everything you can to whimsically and enthusiastically communicate your message because, after all, you are delivering the most important message in the world.

GET FEEDBACK BEFORE YOU PREACH IT

There is a relatively huge mistake that a lot of pastors make on a routine basis. They preach their message without running the material by anyone first. This can be an enormous problem because if you are the only one seeing your content you may miss something because we all have blind spots. You may think something makes perfect sense when it really doesn't. You may think the points connect to the main idea when they really don't. You may be on the right track but need a little guidance to make sure your message connects powerfully to your audience.

For these reasons I suggest utilizing a *preaching team*. What is a preaching team? It is just a group of people you select to help you build your messages. They could help you by looking over what you've put together as I'm suggesting here. Or you could have a more robust preaching team that is with you in the initial stages of content development and anything in between. Perhaps your team could be a trusted friend with whom you share what you've written and talk through your content and then ask for any thoughts on it. I explain the steps to form your preaching team in chapter two of my book *Preaching Killer Sermons*.

No matter how you choose to build your team, I suggest at a minimum that you let someone check out your outline and talk them through it and ask them questions along the way. Especially if you are new to preaching, you'll want to make sure you are not the only one seeing your content before you preach it.

REHEARSE, REHEARSE, REHEARSE

We're almost there! By this point you've worked through all the writing steps. Now it's time to begin rehearsing your sermon. By "rehearsing" I mean practicing delivering your message aloud. In the same way that preaching your message without seeking feedback is dangerous, preaching your message without rehearsing can be equally dangerous.

The first time these words are coming out of your mouth in this way and in this order should *not* be in front of your listeners on Sunday. You should work through the rough parts, the bumpy transitions, the points that don't connect once you say them aloud *before* you get up in front of people. I've provided an extensive guide to rehearsing your sermons in the next chapter.

PRAY AND LISTEN TO GOD

This is the most important step of your sermon writing process. I have made it the last step, but it is really the first step, the second step, and so on. It is *every* step. Meaning, you should pray through the entire process and lean on the Holy Spirit for guidance. I firmly believe that sermon writing is supernatural work that requires supernatural guidance by the Holy Spirit.

All the work put into preparing and writing a sermon is designed to be a Holy Spirit-guided process. God works best in us and through us as we pray, listen, write, repeat. Let me encourage you with this: If you have to omit some steps for the sake of time or otherwise, do *not* omit this step. Make prayer a priority with every step you take in your sermon preparation.

The work of the Holy Spirit and rigorous sermon preparation work hand in hand because God can and does speak to you just as well on Tuesday afternoon as he does on Saturday night. Prepare well, put in the time, and know that God is speaking to you every step of the way. The question is: Are you listening?

CHAPTER FIVE

Preach What You Practice
Why Rehearsing Is Essential to Great Sermon Delivery

I paced the floor as I practiced the words I was going to say. Later that day I was going to have a tough meeting and an even harder conversation with a family at our church that had some concerns with my ministry. I was not looking forward to it because we were dealing with heavy conflict that had arisen in our church, and I had found myself at the center of it.

I'm not a huge fan of confrontation. In fact, if I can avoid it, I will. But in this case there was no getting around it, I had to have this conversation and it was happening in a few hours.

So, I practiced saying what I was going to say. I thought it through, prayed about it, and even recorded myself saying it into the voice memo app on my phone so I could hear what it was going to sound like and make necessary adjustments.

When the time came for the meeting I was ready to be in the moment and engage. Why? Because I wasn't worried about what I was going to say. I had carefully planned that. I was free to feel the moment and insert my thoughts carefully where appropriate.

The meeting ended up being a turning point in my relationship with that family. Our relationship healed and became stronger than it ever was before. What allowed me to face this difficult meeting with ease was rehearsing.

I am a firm believer in rehearsing when what I am going to say is important and has the potential for impact. This practice has the most importance when I preach.

Every time I preach I have an opportunity to fulfill my God-given calling to impact lives with the truth of God's Word and the hope of the gospel.

Every time you preach you have the same opportunity and responsibility. But the effectiveness of our preaching is impacted by a host of variables we cannot control, including distractions in the room. But there is something we can control, and that is how well we prepare.

I find one of the most often-neglected aspects of effective sermon preparation is rehearsing the sermon. By rehearsing I mean preaching the entire message by yourself, or to a handful of people, before you actually preach the sermon to your church.

The reasons behind the reluctance to rehearse are varied. Some preachers might think it's awkward to preach to themselves. They're totally right, by the way. It *is* awkward, but that does not mean you shouldn't do it. Other preachers might avoid it because they don't think it's necessary. Still others may simply have never thought of it. Whatever the case, it is important to work through these obstacles and press forward into a good rehearsing rhythm.

WHY YOU SHOULD REHEARSE YOUR SERMONS

I want to show you the three reasons I believe the often-neglected step of rehearsing the sermon is essential to great sermon delivery.

Rehearsing allows you to know exactly what to expect. The first time words are coming out of your mouth for a particular sermon should not be when you are preaching live to your church. There are too many unforeseeable variables that can go wrong. You may have too much content and end up preaching too long because you didn't know how long that hilarious story about your first date with your wife was actually going to take. Your transitions and segues from one thought to another may make complete sense in your head but fall completely apart when you try to put them into spoken words. Rehearsing allows you to know ahead of time how it will all come together and what the holes are.

It is the same principle that causes your worship leader to rehearse the same song 57 times before singing it once on Sunday… a song that someone else wrote, a song that will take five minutes to play, and that they've probably played before. Why do worship leaders go through this much effort? To make sure they know *exactly* what to expect on Sunday. This allows them to lead without distraction because they're able to focus on the moment rather than trying to remember the next chord.

Your sermon preparation will benefit you and your congregation in much the same way when you rehearse. This does not mean the Holy Spirit doesn't lead you in the moment. It means that you prepare well enough so that you are free to follow the Spirit's leading instead of obsessing over your next thought.

Rehearsing allows you to work out any inconsistencies between your notes, your slides, and your brain. You use a different part of your brain when you read than when you listen, and you use another part when you speak. If you think about it, preparing a sermon without rehearsing uses one part of your brain – reading. You read the words you wrote. Then you get up and speak those words so that your church can listen to them. Two-thirds of your editing brain power is used in the moment instead of ahead of time in rehearsal – speaking and listening. One of the best benefits of rehearsing is that it allows you to use a three-dimensional approach to evaluate how your sermon is coming across – reading it, speaking it out, and listening to how it sounds.

Also, while your brain is busy processing your sermon content from three different angles, you are able to determine if your slides are consistent with your content. When I rehearse I almost always find that one of my slides is out of sync with my sermon at a given moment. Rehearsing allows me to correct this ahead of time. Then it's important to rehearse it once again – at least the part you corrected – to make sure the adjustment you made to your slides was right.

Rehearsing allows you to stay on time. One of the most distracting habits some preachers have is announcing to the church when they are running out of time. "I need to hurry… I'm almost out of time… we're running long… just a few more minutes."

Thinking out loud in this way to let the church know you're feeling rushed and hurried because you have too much content and didn't plan well is terribly bad form. Your listeners do not need to be thinking about the clock. That's *your* job, and it's your job to keep it to yourself so they can focus on the content and on what God is teaching them through the preaching of his Word. If you rehearse you'll know ahead of time if you have too much content. This empowers you beforehand to decide what stays and what goes.

Those are the three reasons I rehearse every sermon I preach. There are arguably more reasons, and the importance of rehearsing cannot be overstated, but those three are the biggest reasons. Now, let's talk about how to rehearse for the greatest benefit.

HOW TO REHEARSE YOUR SERMONS

Rehearsing does not have to be complicated. I hope to simplify the process with some helpful tips and tricks to get you started and accustomed to a habit of rehearsing each sermon. Eventually, rehearsing will become so much a part of your sermon preparation routine that you won't even have to think about it much. But, to get you started it is important to plan it out and think about how you're going to do it practically speaking. I've outlined this in four steps.

(1) *Find a private room where you are comfortable preaching at full volume and expression.* Finding the right space is important because you do not want to be distracted by the thought that others may be listening and wondering why you're talking to yourself. In a previous church I served in I would go to a room upstairs that was not used during the week. I could project my voice at full volume without

wondering who was listening. My office walls were too thin to do this there.

If possible, it's great to rehearse in the auditorium where your church meets if you can get in during the week when no one is around. At my current church we do a staff service on Wednesday where the person who is preaching actually delivers the upcoming Sunday message to the staff. This may be an option for you if you can arrange it. Whichever way you structure it, the key is to make sure the environment is conducive and that everyone there knows what's going on.

(2) *Bring your slides, notes, and anything else you'll have with you when you preach.* To get the most out of your rehearsal time you want to have everything you will use on Sunday. I bring my notes (although I don't look at them when I'm delivering the actual sermon) and my Bible. I recreate my stage setup by placing my computer to my left with my slides on it to function like the onstage monitor that I use on Sundays.

Think through all the tools and aids you'll use when delivering your message and re-create that for your rehearsal. The key is to rehearse with everything as close to the way it will be on Sunday as possible.

(3) *Set up to record using the Voice Memo app on your phone or another recorder.* Recording your rehearsal is vital. I cannot stress this enough. Recording it gives you the ability to listen to yourself and make necessary adjustments that you would not notice otherwise. I use the Voice Memo app on my phone. This allows me to listen back through it and make adjustments. It also helps me recall my sermon in detail when I listen to it early Sunday morning while I'm getting ready for the day. The way you record doesn't matter – you may choose video or like me, simple audio, but the point is to have it captured so you can listen to it as part of your final preparation.

(4) *Preach the entire sermon using your slides and notes as you would when you preach.* Now that you have everything assembled and ready to go, put it all together and preach the message as if there is a room full of people. Use your slides and your notes like it's game day. Pay attention to how your notes and slides line up with what you're saying. Make sure everything is consistent. For example, you may find that a slide stays up way too long after you are on to another point because you don't have another one to turn to just yet.

Make a note of these discrepancies so you can adjust later. Sometimes I make the adjustments while I'm rehearsing because, after all, no one is listening but me. And that's the huge benefit of rehearsing. I would much rather catch the mistakes and make the necessary changes ahead of time. I'm sure you would too.

HOW TO EVALUATE YOUR REHEARSAL

After you've put in the hard work of rehearsing, you want to get the most out of it by evaluating your rehearsal. I've provided some important questions to consider when evaluating your recorded content. You may have different ones, but these will get you thinking. If you rehearse in front of anyone else like we do at our staff service, these questions will help them give you useful feedback as well.

Is the sermon on time or do you need to cut content? A huge benefit of rehearsing is that you get an accurate estimate of how long the sermon is going to take. If you've been allotted 35 minutes for your message and your rehearsal goes 43 minutes, then it's a good idea to cut 8 minutes. Seldom does your sermon actually take less when you preach it on Sunday than it did in rehearsal. Most preachers generally end up going longer the day of, so you'll want to decide ahead of time what needs to go and what should stay.

Does your content flow well and make sense? Listen back through your transitions from one point to another. Does it connect and make logical sense? When you go from one thought to another, will your listeners be able to track with you? The way to do this is listen for connecting words and phrases. Are you taking people along on a journey or leaving them to find their way to wherever you go next?

Do your slides match what you're saying at every point in the message? As I mentioned before, I almost always have a slide that hangs out too long. Typically I've moved on, but the slide is still hanging out on the screen even though it does not relate to what I'm saying at the moment. This is easily fixed, so just look out for it and correct it. You may find that the thought you moved on to would really benefit from having a slide dedicated to it. These issues are often missed when writing the sermon, which is why rehearsing is so important.

How does it sound when you say it? Does a part need to be rewritten? Our content can look great on paper, but when we say it we realize it doesn't quite connect the way we had planned when we wrote it. Where in the rehearsal did you feel like it wasn't quite right? Work on rewriting those parts and be sure to practice them again.

How are you interacting with your notes? Do they match what you're saying? Do your notes need to be adjusted? In a later chapter I'll show you how to ditch your notes altogether.

But if you're using notes as part of your sermon delivery process make sure they're accurate and that you're keeping your interaction with them to a minimum. If you're referring to your notes as you go, are they in order and helpful? These are pointers to make note of during rehearsal and adjust as needed. This will prevent you from being in the middle of your message on Sunday and realizing that your notes are confusing you and causing you to lose your bearings.

Do you need to jot down that extra illustration you thought of while rehearsing? Invariably I will have sudden inspiration hit me during rehearsal – a story to tell, an illustration that fits perfectly. I'm sure this happens to you too. When it does, be sure to write it down and adjust your plan accordingly. On a related note, when inspiration hits you always write it down with plenty of detail! Never rely on your memory. I have learned the hard way on this one as I ended up forgetting illustrations and stories that I was sure I would never forget.

Does this sermon fire you up? Will you feel passionate about it on Sunday? Rehearsing allows you to get a taste of preaching the content ahead of time and see how it makes you feel to preach it. If it does nothing for you, see what needs to change in it (or change in you) before Sunday to make sure that you're preaching with authentic passion. Few things work in your favor more than when you're passionate about your message and it shows.

Finally, I listen to my recording on Sunday morning while clicking through my slides to give myself one last refresher before preaching. I'm a firm believer in this process because I've seen it work to improve my own preaching and that of so many preachers I've helped.

It's great to couple rehearsing your sermons with evaluating them as well. When you combine rehearsing ahead of time and evaluating afterward, it's the one-two-punch of improving your sermon prep and delivery process.

WATCH YOUR GAME FILM

When you watch your game film and evaluate your message you are able to see what others are seeing when they watch your message. You catch your common mistakes and physical distractions (more on those in chapter eleven). You see what you can do to improve for the next message. I want to give you some practical points to help you evaluate your message video.

Look at your gestures and movement. Are your hand gestures and physical movements consistent with what you're saying? Are your movements purposeful and intentional? To see how your movements look on their own, play the video without audio and just watch your movements. Do they look natural and smooth? Mastering good stage movements and gestures can help you drastically improve receptiveness to your preaching.

There are a variety of other considerations to evaluate. Are you messing with your microphone in a distracting way? Are you using filler words and audible pauses? (More on those points of evaluation in chapter eleven.) Are you keeping the audience engaged? How are your transitions from one thought to another? Are you relying too much on your notes? (See how to ditch the notes entirely in chapter thirteen.) What is working about your presentation? What is really connecting with your audience? Why? How can you build on what is good and work on what is bad in your presentation?

The key is to evaluate each sermon with the aim of getting better for the next one. Don't harp on the bad things. Learn from them and improve them for your next sermon. Over time, if you make this a habit, you will see yourself become a more natural speaker.

PART TWO
MASTER THE SECRET WEAPONS

CHAPTER SIX

Once Upon A Time
How Storytelling Changes Everything

I'm not the most athletic person in the world. That's a bit of an understatement, I'm not an athletic person at all. I try to remain active and fit, but I do activities that don't require athletic coordination like walking on a treadmill and lifting weights.

Even with my limitations, when I was in elementary and middle school I tried my hand at a few different sports. I grew up in a small town in Oklahoma and sports was a near requirement for every guy. I tried baseball, basketball, track, soccer, and karate.

But the sport I loved the most was football. I loved football because I discovered that in my position as a defensive end I didn't need to know how to catch or throw the ball, I didn't need to know intricate plays, and I didn't even need all that much athletic coordination.

I didn't need all this because I discovered one secret weapon I had: I was relentlessly aggressive. I focused on getting around the blocker and sacking the quarterback. Every snap of the ball was a new opportunity to figure out a way to break through the line or skirt around it and nail the quarterback before he was able to pass or hand off the ball.

This was my secret weapon and it enabled me to focus on the one or two things I could do that would get the biggest results.

Much like my experience in football, public speaking has two secret weapons. If you master these two weapons you'll become virtually unstoppable as a content presenter of any kind – but especially as a preacher. When it comes to mastering your preaching game, you really can't fully maximize your impact until you become proficient using these two weapons of sermon delivery. So what are these two weapons that take your preaching to the next level? They are storytelling and humor.

I'll tell you something that I probably should not say: If you master the art of telling a gripping story that captures and moves your audience and you master the ability to be truly funny, then you can actually break a lot of communication "rules" and still have a tremendously impactful sermon. This does not mean I am suggesting that you throw out the best-practices presented in this book and other good preaching books. Rather, I'm saying that effective storytelling and humor are such powerful tools for capturing and moving your audience that they have the potential to make up for lack in other areas. This is why you should try to deepen your skill level in these two areas.

In the next few chapters I will drill down on these two areas and reveal actionable insights and best-practices that you can begin to implement in your next sermon. Let's dive in by first looking at why you should tell stories in your sermons.

WHY YOU SHOULD USE STORIES IN YOUR MESSAGES

In some preaching communities there exists a sort of aversion to storytelling. In these circles it is largely thought that storytelling is somehow a lesser version of preaching that lacks the true substance – the meat – we are to feed the mature in our flocks. There is a bit of a juxtaposition between those who masterfully grip their audience with storytelling and those who masterfully grip their audience with exposition of the text. It is thought that these two parties cannot intermingle and are opposed to each other.

This is a false dichotomy because the church needs both! We need preachers who can accurately divide the word of truth *and* know how to grip their listeners with story. For this reason, I want to spend some time making the case for why you should tell stories in your sermons. I want to show you that it is not a lesser form of preaching. Rather, it is a tool that, if used well, can yield massive results toward life-change. What are the reasons we should use stories in our preaching?

Most of the Bible is narrative. Maybe God is onto something. When God wanted to reveal his character, his will, and his Word he used mostly narrative to do it. He tells us the story of his people throughout much of the Old Testament. In seeing the tendencies of the people of Israel we see ourselves. We see how God related to them, how he was patient with them but also jealous for a people who belonged to him but were routinely turning their backs on him.

In that story we see so much that we could not see so vividly if God had merely given a list of commandments to follow. Fortunately, we got the commandments and the story. The commandments are given context within a story. Our sermons would do well to follow the same pattern. Show the precepts of God in the context of the story of God.

Jesus told stories more than he "taught" propositional truth. One of Jesus' most common methods of teaching was to ask questions and tell stories. He was masterful at getting to the heart of the situation by telling a parable or using a metaphor that explained truth so much more powerfully than a set of propositional truths ever could. His tendency to use parables and ask questions and give metaphors made his teaching memorable and repeatable such that we still easily recall Jesus' stories without having to reference where they're recorded.

How many times have you heard people refer to "The Prodigal Son" who may not even know that story is part of three parallel parables in Luke 15 that all point to the relentless love of the Father that causes him to pursue his children even when they're wayward?

Jesus could easily have just taught the truth that God loves us with a relentless pursuit. He could have explained all the reasons why we know this to be true from a theological perspective. He could have given three reasons why God chooses to love in that way. But instead he chose to show us in the set of three stories – the lost coin, the lost sheep, and the lost son – that sink so much deeper into our hearts and minds. We cannot escape the reality of the story. Jesus was a masterful storyteller and the impact is lasting.

People naturally tune into stories. If you've preached for any length of time you've had this experience: Half way through your sermon you look out to your audience and it hits you – you've lost them. They are there but not *really* there. There is a lull in your message, and you realize that to have any hope of recovery you must do something to recapture your listeners' attention. What do you do?

Here's what I do in these moments. I tell a story. There is nothing like launching into a story to make heads that were once down glued to a phone pop back up and attend to what you're saying. No one wants to miss a story. They want to know what happened. By telling stories you capture people that you may have lost. Gaining back attention is not the only goal of storytelling. Stories are powerful apart from any attention-grabbing mechanism, but that is a huge part of their benefit.

People listen to stories as if they are first-hand experiences. When you tell a story it has a profound impact on your listeners as they naturally place themselves in the story as if it is their own experience. A study cited by Harrie Truscott in an article entitled *Why Do We Love Stories?* shows this. Truscott states:

> "Many years ago, a team of scientists discovered a neurological connection between stories and the area of the brain which is responsible for empathy... These feelings... tend to increase when we are told stories which resonate with us.... [N]eurologists have also shown that our brains become more active when we are told a story. Normally, the 'language processing' region of the brain would light up when we take in new information. However, when infor-

mation is delivered in the form of a story, other areas become activated as well, such as the sensory cortex and motor cortex. These are the parts of the brain typically triggered when we experience events firsthand."[4]

This is an astounding phenomenon to consider as a preacher. When you tell a story, it causes your listeners to place *themselves* in the story. When people have placed themselves in the story you are telling, you have a great deal of leverage to influence them and persuade them. A fundamental aspect of communication is persuasion. Stories well told can help you be more persuasive and, as a result, have more influence.

Stories have the ability to stir emotions in a way that other forms of communication do not. Have you ever seen NBC's hit show *This Is Us?* To give you the general theme of the show, I could tell you, "The relationship between a parent and a child is complex and nuanced and becomes even more pronounced as the child enters adulthood and the relationship changes over time." That's a true statement, and it's what the show is about. But you are likely not moved by it.

Go watch one episode of *This Is Us* and you'll see the theme illustrated in a powerful way because you'll be

---

[4] Why Do We Love Stories? by Harrie Truscott
(https://www.youandco.com.au/blog/why-we-love-stories)

watching the story and not just hearing a description. You'll place yourself in the story and feel it deeply. In fact, I dare you not to shed a tear! My wife and I cry every single episode. Why? The story brings us in. We connect with the characters and begin to care about them. Yes, we know they're fictional, but that doesn't matter. The story is powerful enough to cause us to empathize – to place ourselves in the story – and feel things as if they are happening to us or to people we love.

It is important to understand a story can have this kind of impact on people. In my book *Preaching Killer Sermons,* I discussed the importance of pathos in communication. Pathos is a way of describing when audience members are moved at an emotional level by a speaker. Aristotle theorized that communication has three primary elements: ethos, a trustworthy speaker; pathos, a message that stirs emotion; and logos, a message that makes sense.

The pathos element is crucial to get people to care about the logos. In other words, until people feel something they don't care about knowing it. This is where stories come in. Tell a great story that moves people emotionally and you'll cause them to lean in closer and want to hear more.

HOW TO USE STORIES IN YOUR SERMONS

At this point I'm sure you can see there a variety of reasons why you should use stories in your sermons. Stories are an effective way to capture and maintain interest in your content. But how do you actually tell a story? Is every story told the same way? Is every story told for the same reason? Like many principles of communication, there is much freedom in how storytelling is practiced.

Within that freedom I want to give you some of the best ways to use stories in your messages. It's important to nail down how you're going to use a particular story in a sermon. It's important to know where it fits in your message and how it will serve your main idea. There are four basic ways you can use a story.

Tell a story to build ethos. Remember, in Aristotle's theory of effective communication ethos is the number-one element. This simply means that the speaker needs to prove him or herself a trustworthy deliverer of content. This trust-building is especially important when you preach.

When you tell a story for the purpose of ethos-building it helps you establish rapport with your audience by letting them in on something about you on a personal level. Maybe your story is a bit self-deprecating or shows your humanity. This can be a powerful way to build trust and allow your listeners to see you as a believable person. This is the easiest type of story to tell because you don't have to make the story fit your content as you would most other stories you tell during a sermon. In this case the point of the story is the story itself. You can make it fit if you want, but that falls into the second category, which is to use a story as an introduction to your message.

Use a story to intro the sermon. In this case you use the story to introduce the sermon itself and build tension for your topic. There is a lot of freedom here because you can make just about any story fit as long as you connect the point or "aha!" moment of the story with the tension of the message.

Here's what I mean. I gave a sermon recently about the story in John 21 where Jesus told the disciples to cast the net on the other side of the boat after they had been fishing all night and had caught nothing. They obeyed even though it probably seemed ridiculous to them. They had to be thinking, "We know what we're doing! Besides, if the fish aren't on this side of the boat, what makes you think they're going to be on the other side of the boat!" But, as you know, they threw the net and caught 153 fish – enough for a charcoal breakfast on the beach prepared by Jesus himself!

My opening story to that sermon was about when I had been going to the gym just piddling around for several months. It was mundane, routine, and monotonous. Not surprising, I was not getting the results I wanted. A friend told me about a program that focused on four core workouts: squats, deadlifts, overhead press, and bench press. I balked at it at first because it seemed so simplistic.

How are those lifts any different from what I've been doing? What good will that do? But I figured, "Why not give it a try? I'm bored in the gym anyway." Within a week I saw results!

From there I went on to talk about different ways that same principle applies in other parts of our lives. This made it easy to pivot to the bottom line of my message: When we trust Jesus with the ordinary he produces the extraordinary. Weight-lifting has nothing to do with John 21, but it doesn't have to relate to it to be an effective example. That's the beauty of a story. As long as you can tie it together in a way that is connectable and reasonable to your audience, it can be a powerful way to open your message.

Use a story to illustrate a point. There are lots of ways to illustrate a point, but there is no better way than a good story. A story well told has the effect of putting flesh on the bones of your message. A story can make a point come alive in living color to your audience. The idea here is much the same as using a story to introduce the sermon. This can be particularly effective when you need to bring your audience back in to paying attention to you. What I find effective is to state the point and then jump right into a story that illustrates it. The best stories are those that are true and about your life.

You should make sure this is varied to keep it interesting to your audience. For example, if every story is about your kids it starts to get old, especially to those who do not have kids and have a hard time relating. Keep it fresh, vary it up, and you'll find that your points will sink down deeper into your listeners' hearts and minds. In the next chapter I'll share more about how to come up with stories and how to structure them to illustrate a point well.

Use a story to wrap up your sermon. You may use a story to tie your sermon in a bow and let it sink into people's hearts in a powerful way by telling a story at the end. What works powerfully here is to tell a story that makes people feel something. When your listeners feel, they are open, and when they are open, life-change can happen. I have found it helpful to start a story at the beginning of the sermon and leave it hanging, like a cliffhanger, through the message. Then, finish the story at the end. When this is done well your message feels like a completed journey to your listeners and they are grateful for the ride.

There are many reasons to use stories in your sermons and many ways in which you can use them effectively. In the next chapter we'll dive into the nitty gritty detail of how to tell stories for maximum impact in your sermons.

CHAPTER SEVEN

It Matters How You Tell It
The Nitty Gritty of Storytelling

I recently preached a message that was full of what I considered great teaching content and biblical exposition. But the one thing people remembered was a story I told about a miscarriage my wife and I experienced. It wasn't necessarily the point of the message, but it was definitely the takeaway: *This is what it looks like to trust God through difficult times.* It turns out that takeaway was the desired response I was aiming for, but it was communicated differently from how I had planned. People leaned in and connected with the story. They related the message to their own experience not because of the points I made but because of the story. That story was powerful enough to stand on its own and be remembered by everyone there. Long after they forget the points, many of them will recall that story.

Why is this the case? Why is storytelling such an effective and lasting part of communication? The importance of storytelling in communication cannot be overstated. In a Wired.com article entitled "The Art of Immersion: Why We Tell Stories," Frank Rose describes how stories play a central role in the human experience:

> "Just as the brain detects patterns in the visual forms of nature – a face, a figure, a flower – and in sound, so too it detects patterns in information. Stories are recognizable patterns, and in those patterns we find meaning. We use stories to make sense of our world and to share that understanding with others. They are the signal within the noise."[5]

Consider what Rose is arguing in that statement. Stories serve to give people patterns by which they can find meaning. If people use stories to make sense of their world, they will use stories to make sense of your sermons. This means if you want people to understand and apply your message, communicating its truths in story form should be a substantial part of how you give your message.

---

[5] The Art of Immersion: Why Do We Tell Stories By Frank Rose (https://www.wired.com/2011/03/why-do-we-tell-stories/)

Beyond that, when Rose says that people share the understanding they gain from stories with others, it rings true in the realm of preaching. How many times have you preached an entire message and the only thing people commented on was the story you told? When they tell others about your message they will recount the story to them as well. Why? Your story helps them make sense of their world, of their faith, and, if done effectively, of God and their relationship to him.

In that same article Rose goes on to say: "We know this much: People want to be immersed. They want to get involved in a story, to carve out a role for themselves, to make it their own."[6] Since we know stories are incredible teaching tools, we should become lifelong students of how to master the art of telling great stories. How do we structure and tell stories in our messages that immerse people and give them the optimal chance to find meaning, connect with divine truth, and ultimately experience life-change?

In this chapter, we will dig into the ins and outs of effective storytelling. We will discover how you can begin utilizing stories effectively in your messages so that you can see first-hand how much impact your stories can have on your audience.

---

[6] The Art of Immersion: Why Do We Tell Stories By Frank Rose (https://www.wired.com/2011/03/why-do-we-tell-stories/)

FINDING STORIES TO TELL

Before we can dig into the nitty gritty of how to create and tell a story I want to give you some practical ways to find stories to tell in your messages. Great stories are all around you. You just have to have eyes to see them and develop the skill of capturing everyday events and turning them into powerful, funny, motivating, or even just amusing stories you can use in your messages.

The best thing you can do when you develop a story to tell is to file it away to use again at a later time. More on using your stories multiple times later, but for now it is important to understand that the process I will show you can and should be repeated over and over until you have a big pile of stories that are well-crafted and ready to be applied to almost any sermon you deliver. As we explore how to find stories, keep in mind that you should duplicate this process for each story.

There are a plethora of places you can find great stories to tell. Some of these include stories from history, stories from current news and events, and stories of people in your church. But for the purposes of mastering storytelling in your sermons, I want to drill down on the best place you can find stories – your own life.

THE NEVER-ENDING WELL OF YOUR LIFE

The absolute best place to find great stories to tell is your own life. The stories from your life and your experiences will far outshine any other stories you could tell in almost every case. This is not because your stories are necessarily better, but when you tell your story, it's powerful and intriguing and has the best chance of accomplishing the powerful results that a story should accomplish in a sermon. Let's dig into all the myriad ways you can plumb the never-ending well of your life and draw out a bucket of stories.

Your major life events. A great first step to building out a catalogue of stories to tell is to think back through your life and make a list of every major life event you've gone through. These don't have to be profound because you can develop a profound truth from just about any event. What memories do you have as a child? What are some funny things that happened when you were growing up? What are some tragic things you had to go through? What are your memories of family life, school, activities, sports? Did you move several times? Did you grow up in a small town or was it a big city? Are your parents still together or is their divorce a part of your story? With every question consider whether this is a life-event or circumstance or situation that could later be developed into a story.

When was your first crush? What did you do in high school? Did you get into trouble? Were you the good kid? Where did you attend college? What was it like? The questions could go on and on. There is literally no end to how deep the stories can go. If it seems like you're compiling a long list keep in mind that you are building up a lifetime of sermon storytelling fodder. No list is too long.

Your God story. As preachers, we should be able to clearly and compellingly articulate the story of how we came to faith in Christ. What was your life like before you met Jesus? How did you meet Jesus? What is your life like since you surrendered to Jesus? Knowing how to tell your story of faith is powerful when preaching.

But consider your God story that is ongoing and constant. How has God continued to work in your life? What were the events and circumstances that led you to pursue ministry? Were you open to the calling initially? Did you fight it? How has your walk with God progressed throughout your spiritual life? Write down every major God moment you've had. The sum total of your life with God is your testimony, and that is among the most powerful stories you can tell.

Stories drawn from your marriage. If you are married, your love story and all of its parts can be very interesting to people. How did you meet your spouse? What did you do on your first date? How did you propose? Where did you get married? What have been your challenges? What have been your high points? What are the lessons learned, and what events helped you learn those lessons? What do you fight about? It's important to get permission from your spouse before using stories about your marriage, but at this point we are just compiling a list.

Stories about your kids. I have three daughters four years old and younger. Every single day is a wealth of opportunities to capture stories from the things they say and do. If you have kids it doesn't matter if they are young or grown up and out of your house. Think through experiences and events in your kids' lives. They might be profound and weighty. They can also be light-hearted and funny. Make a list of everything your kids have said, done, participated in, and experienced.

Much like stories about your marriage, your kids should have the right to veto any story they'd rather you not tell. No story is worth damaging your child or betraying trust. Every kid is different. One kid may not mind the extra attention that comes with being the center of a story. To other kids it could be mortifying. It's hard enough to be a pastor's kid, so be careful not to sacrifice your kids on the altar of a good story.

Your everyday life. Finally, when developing a catalogue of stories to tell you should make a list of every single thing you experience, observe, and participate in throughout your everyday life. This could be anything from driving, to interacting with friends, neighbors, and co-workers, shopping, working, going to the gym, brushing your teeth, mowing your lawn, etc. The beauty of it is there is absolutely no area of life from which a story cannot be derived.

Ministry experiences. In the course of pastoring people a plethora of interesting things happen. Sometimes these are funny as they demonstrate the potential for silliness that church people have. Other times they are heartbreaking as they show the fallenness of humanity. Still other times they demonstrate the ins and outs of living life on mission as a pastor. These stories can let your listeners into the realities of your day-to-day ministry experiences. There are cautions associated with these kinds of stories. Make sure to see my list of must-do's later in this chapter to make sure you avoid some pitfalls in this area.

At this point you have a long list of potential stories from several different areas of your life. What do you do with that list? How does a life-event or something your child said or your last shopping trip turn into a sermon-ready story? Let me show you the steps required to take anything from your life and make it a story.

STEPS TO BUILDING A STORY IN YOUR SERMON

In addition to creating a lengthy list of potential stories, we've also explored where to place the story in your sermon. Once you know where it should be placed and how it fits in your sermon you'll be able to start working on how to tell it. Let's look at the steps in building a great story.

Start with the end in mind. When you set out to develop a story to tell in your sermon, you should begin by asking: "What is the point of this story?" Most importantly, what you want to do in this step is make sure the story is going to accomplish what you want it to accomplish whether that is illustrate a point, drive home an important idea, make people feel something deeply, make people laugh and lighten up a bit, build tension, introduce your sermon's main idea, or wrap up your message.

Work backwards to determine what people need to know. Once you know the end-goal of the story, begin to work backwards from that point and think through all the steps that will be needed to make your story work. To do this, you need to answer some questions that will help you determine which direction to take the story.

These may include: What do people need to know to understand the point of the story? What are the events that lead up to the setting of the story? What details are important for people to know? What details are not important? Who is in the story? What is the setting? What happened? When did it happen? What moment in time do I need to bring people into so that they can fully immerse themselves in this story? Why does it matter?

Outline the main parts of the story. Once you have determined where the story is going (its point) and what people need to know to arrive at that point, begin outlining the main parts of the story. Every story has a setting (a scenario, a situation), some dialogue or events, some point of tension or conflict, a resolution of that tension, and a conclusion.

A story in a sermon may break the rules especially when it is intended only to illustrate a point and not necessarily to stand on its own. So don't get hung up on trying to make every story fit a story arc and be screenplay-ready. Rather, focus on the journey the story will take people on to arrive at the end point you want for them.

Write out the story. Once you have an outline it's time to build it out and write the story. This is a tedious step for a lot of us who would rather just tell the story. But it is so important to capture and convey *exactly* how you want the story to feel and flow. The best way to do this is to write it down.

Some of my best go-to stories that have paid the biggest dividends in my sermons are stories that I took time to write out in detail. This also helps me internalize the stories so that when I tell them I know exactly how they should flow from one part to another. It also helps for nailing comedic timing, which we will deal with in the next chapter.

When writing out a story I find it helps to consider how I'm utilizing what I call the three F-words of great storytelling. First, the *Feels*. Stories cause us to empathize, so it's a great opportunity to draw out emotion and help people feel something. Ask yourself: Where is the emotion in this story and how can I convey it?

Second, the *Funny*. People are paying attention when you tell a story, so make them laugh. It will build credibility for you and put them at ease. Ask: What are the humorous part of this story that I can pull out?

Third, the *Fail*. Stories that demonstrate how someone met a challenge, made mistakes, and ultimately overcame go a long way as people put themselves in the story and often relate better to imperfection than to perfection. Ask: How can I demonstrate real humanity in this story?

Cut unnecessary details. Now that you've written out the story, it is important to cut any unnecessary details that bog the story down. You could go back through the questions you've asked and drill down on the negatives: What do people not need to know? What led up to it that is a detail that doesn't matter? Who is in the story that doesn't matter to the point of the story? What in the setting do people really not need to know in order to understand the setting of the story?

The point is to make it lean. If it isn't necessary to the overall story, cut it. We've all heard someone tell a story where half the details are boring and unnecessary. You want to avoid this by thinking through what should be cut ahead of time. Why are many scenes deleted from a given movie before its release? If a scene doesn't serve the plot, it has to go. The same should be true for your stories. Keep them tight and focused.

Rehearse the story. I cannot emphasize enough how important it is to rehearse the story before you put it in your sermon. The goal of rehearsing is not memorization but rather internalization. Just as you should internalize your messages so that you can preach without notes (more on that in chapter thirteen), you should rehearse your stories so that they sink deep inside your heart and mind and you can tell them just as you planned, powerfully and effectively, anytime you want. Rehearsing ensures that your story comes together and lands where you need it to land. Rehearsing stories also keeps you from letting the story go too long so that your sermon runs over your allotted time. You can read more on how to rehearse your story and the entire sermon in chapter five.

MUST DO'S OF STORYTELLING

As we have discussed, storytelling in a sermon can be incredibly powerful, but it is important to follow some best-practices. I want to offer three must-dos of storytelling.

Jump right in. As when you illustrate a point, you do *not* need to give metadata. In other words, you should not announce that a story is coming. "I'm going to tell you a story. This is a good story. It's one that has a great moral to it. Here is the story." What I just did there… Don't do that! By the time you actually start telling the story you will have lost your listeners. Just tell the story. People realize instantly when you transition from teaching didactically to telling a story. They'll tune in and you'll get more traction if you waste no time jumping into it.

Make sure the connection to your content is clear. The beauty of stories is that virtually any story can help illustrate any point. But this is only the case if you make the connection clear. A story may be interesting to your audience, but if the connection to your content is foggy, you will have just told a good story ... that will not have any impact on the outcome of your message. To ensure that the connection is made, think through the part of your story that is the most significant to you and make sure that you make that connection perceptible to your audience. If you are merely telling the story for the purpose of building ethos with your listeners, make sure that is clear as well.

Build tension (sometimes let it sit). Every story should have some tension built in. Tension is what makes a story interesting and worth listening to. Sometimes the tension is minor if the story is light-hearted and brief. In those cases the tension could be as simple as building up an expectation of how the story will turn out only to have a surprise ending.

Another way of building tension is more accurately described as building anticipation. This is what TV producers do masterfully at the end of each episode to get us excited about the upcoming episode. Every story should have bits of tension and anticipation-building that cause listeners to lean in and want to hear more.

Sometimes tension can be even more powerful when you do not resolve it right away but let it sit for a while and then wrap it up at the end of your message. This can bolster the effect of the story as people are left in tension and forced to deal with the unresolved part of the story. I did this in a sermon in which I told a story about some bad news I received from a doctor. I had had some lab work completed, and the results did not look good. The doctor told me I likely had a pretty serious disease that's difficult to treat and impossible to cure. I told my church how it felt to receive this news. I told them how devastated I was in that moment. I told them of the doubts and fears I experienced and the questions I had and the "why me's" that ensued.

Then I moved on with the message. Many people probably wanted to know how things turned out. But the tension of the story worked to support the point of the message. At the end of the sermon I circled back and told them that the doctor was wrong – thank God. I didn't have what he thought I had. My lab work was showing something that could be treated and was not the death sentence he had read to me. Letting the bad news sit for a little while made the message more powerful as people were emotionally connected to the content.

Change or omit names to protect confidences if needed. Anytime your story involves real people be sure to protect them. I find that simply changing names or omitting them altogether takes a step toward keeping the subject of the story from being found out. You can either just say, "A guy I know…" or "A guy, I'll call him Jeff…" This way you're keeping it honest, but everyone knows you are making an effort to conceal identities.

Obscure details to protect confidences. This is a huge one especially if you are telling a fresh story, such as one that recently happened or involved or affected people in your audience. Omit some unnecessary details and be vague where detail is not needed. For example, instead of saying, "A recently divorced man in our church came in for counseling the other day…," you might change that to, "I once spoke with a man dealing with some pain from his former marriage."

In the first opening, the audience is able to narrow this person down to any recently divorced men in our church. If you're that guy you are going to feel like your confidence has been shattered and as though every eye is on you. But in the second opening, it's a man dealing with pain from his past marriage. We don't know if he is part of the church. We don't know when his marriage ended. We don't know when the conversation happened. But those details don't matter to the story. And obscuring them helps people focus not on trying to identify who is being spoken of but rather on the content of the story itself.

Ask permission if you're going to talk about a particular person. If you are not going to omit and obscure names and details to protect confidences, then you should *always* get permission to tell the story. People appreciate having a heads-up and usually are fine with it unless the story is one they'd rather not be told… Or not be told *yet*.

Never assume the person won't see the sermon. When considering whether or not to tell a story, you should always ask yourself this question: *Would I be totally okay with the person I'm referring to being at church that day or watching online?* If the answer is even slightly "no" then make the necessary adjustments to the story to obscure it a bit or leave it out altogether. I've heard some horror stories from pastors I work with who thought that person would never listen to their sermon and hear the story only to realize that they did and it caused a big mess of drama that no preacher wants to deal with. Use your discretion and listen to your intuition. When in doubt, leave it out.

GETTING THE MOST OUT OF ONE STORY

As you build a catalogue of stories it's great to plan how to utilize a story more than once so that you can get the most life out of it. I want to offer a few ways to consider stretching the life of your stories.

Tell it more than once. Simply tell your story more than once. When you get a story polished it can live with you and in your sermons for years to come. It's important not to wear out a story on the same audience, so use some caution here. But, generally speaking, telling the same story multiple times is fine as long as you've let enough time pass in between and perhaps you tell it in a different way each time.

Repurpose your stories. A story can live beyond your Sunday sermon. You can tell the story on your blog or include it in a book you write. Anytime you guest speak to a different audience you can bring in your best stories that you know engage the audience well.

Make a different point with it. As I mentioned earlier, any story can illustrate just about any point. Use this to your advantage by telling the same story but making a different point with it. This allows your stories to live beyond one sermon and one truth applied from them.

Stories are powerful tools, but they are one part of the two secret weapons you must master to maximize your preaching impact. The other secret weapon is using humor, which combines magnificently with storytelling. We'll dive into using humor in your messages in the next chapter.

CHAPTER EIGHT

That Was Hilarious!
Why Humor Is Worth Mastering

My passion for great communication and especially great preaching began when I was in high school. During my sophomore year I attended two Christian summer camps. Both camps had a similar structure. There were activities throughout the day and a worship service each night. Both camps had about the same types of activities and fun things to do. Both had a similar flow at the evening worship services where there would be a video highlight recap of the day, music with a live band, and a message. In both cases the speaker would build on his previous message from the night before and keep the same theme through the week.

Though there were many similarities, the first camp made a lasting impact on me to the point where I still remember specific things the speaker said nearly 20 years later. The other camp was altogether unremarkable. I'm sure that the speaker said some good and right and true things. I just didn't have the same draw to him as I did to the speaker at the first camp. As a result, he didn't make as big an impact on me.

ONE THING MADE ALL THE DIFFERENCE

There was only one difference between these two speakers: *The first speaker was funny, the second one was not.* Humor is powerful. The speaker who used humor well was able to build trust with me, draw me in, and keep me interested in his content in ways the other speaker was not.

In fact, when I think about the preachers and speakers who have not only made the biggest impact on me but are the most well-known preachers around today, almost all of them are funny. I'm not saying they're "silly" or comedians. Rather, I'm saying they are tuned into what makes people laugh and know how and when to use humor as a tool to make their communication more effective.

In this chapter I will reveal how the best speakers in the world use humor to make their communication stick. I've studied this for years now and have experimented in my own preaching to determine how to use humor, when to use it, and what effect it has. You will discover how to overcome any fears you may have, why you should attempt humor, and some immediate ways to get started. First, I want to deal with a common fear all of us have experienced.

DON'T BE AFRAID TO TRY

I want to first address something worth mentioning: *Some public speakers are terrified to attempt humor for fear that if they fail they will humiliate themselves.* My communication professors in college would suggest not even attempting humor because it's too risky. Their argument was that it is better to have a dry, serious, straightforward speech than risk being embarrassed because you attempted to get a laugh but instead got the sound of crickets. At the time, I thought this was lame. Not even attempt it? That seemed overly cautious and timid to me.

But I've realized over time that this is a real fear people have. Think about it, public speaking is often one of the top fears people have in life. Preachers have already found a way to overcome that and subject themselves to the scrutiny of speaking to people. The thought of pressing on that fear to the next level and risk failing while trying to be funny is too much for some people.

In fact, some would argue that stand-up comedy is the most difficult form of public speaking. This is because the audience is watching a stand-up comic for the sole purpose of laughing. If the comic does not deliver, the whole show is a bomb. And no one, not even the most experienced stand-up comedian, is totally free from the fear of bombing.

But here's the great thing: When you preach, humor is merely a small part of the bigger picture; this removes the pressure of typical stand-up comedy. During a sermon, people are not *expecting* to get side-splitting comedy from the preacher. So any bit of laughter-producing comedy is typically viewed as a bonus to the audience but can be a powerful tool for the speaker (more on that later).

For now, keep reading and don't get hung up on the fear of failing. I'm going to show you how to start small and decide what works for you. You'll find your voice that fits you when it comes to humor and discover how to use it well.

WHY USE HUMOR IN SERMONS

You may be asking why would you need to attempt humor in your sermons. What's the point? There are countless benefits of using humor in a sermon, and I think knowing the "why" of humor will help motivate you to put in the necessary time and energy to develop the skill of using it in your preaching. Here are some of the most important ones.

Laughing puts people at ease. Put yourself in the shoes of a newcomer to your church. Let's say this person is not only new to your church but is coming back to church for the first time since childhood. She is a bit skeptical about organized religion and a bit suspicious of church and especially preachers. She has all this going through her mind in addition to the fact that she thinks (no matter how large your church is) that everyone knows she is new. She may even think everyone knows that she is reluctant to be there. She stands there during the music and sits through the announcements. She wonders when it will end and if she made the right decision with her Sunday morning.

Then you step up to speak. There's a lot for you to overcome in her mind. She doesn't think you "get" her, doesn't think you live in the real world and understand real problems. She thinks you work one day a week and piddle in your garden or play golf the other six days. You have to break through those invisible barriers, and humor is one of the best ways to do this.

To the person in our example who is possibly regretting her decision to be there, an unexpected laugh is a gift. This is because it is a release of the nervousness and apprehension she is bottling up inside. It helps her breathe a little, relax, and settle in.

I would bet the last time you really laughed – I'm talking let out a good howler – you weren't thinking about your stresses in that moment. You weren't thinking about deadlines or meetings or bills or your strained relationships. No, in that moment your body released all that tension and allowed you to feel at ease. Chemically what happened was endorphins were released and your body was coated with natural "feel good."

This is a gift from God and also a powerful tool for you to use as a preacher to put even the most skeptical people in your audience at ease and give them an opportunity to relax.

Laughter can be used to relieve tension during an otherwise heavy sermon. I've written before about why it is so important to oscillate between intensity and relief in your messages. I gave an example from a well-known movie producer and the decision he made to do this in one of his films.

I saw an interview with Mel Gibson talking about producing *The Passion of the Christ*. He said the scenes of Jesus' crucifixion were so intense that he knew he had to "hold the viewer's hand through the movie." This is why the movie goes from scenes of intensity to scenes of relief. One scene might be Jesus' being flogged and beaten followed by another scene that shows him with his mother back in time building a chair.

Gibson could have written the movie where it begins intense, remains intense for the entire film, and ends with great intensity. The problem with that approach is that viewers can only take so much. There has to be a balance of intensity and relief.

This principle also applies to preaching. It is especially important to give your listeners periodic relief when you are dealing with hard truths or a challenging topic. Humor well-applied can allow your listeners a break so that when you re-engage them they are ready to hear it.

This is why when I'm coaching people on how to give a best man or maid of honor speech at a wedding I tell them to use the rule of three, which applied this way means: Make them laugh, make them laugh, warm their heart. Laughter followed by serious content is a formula that works. In these cases I try to get them to think of two things about the bride or groom or their relationship that are funny but appropriate and not at all offensive to them. Then I try to get them to think of something about their relationship that is sweet and will get people to react with audible "awwwww."

But doesn't that damage an otherwise serious moment? It can. That's why you have to know when and how to do it, but it's not complicated. Keep reading and I'll deal with that question more as we go.

When you make your listeners laugh it builds trust and makes them like you. Here's a fun little anecdote. My wife and I were friends for two years before we started dating. We met each other through mutual friends and would see each other in the same circles as we hung out with friends as single people. My wife did not take an interest in me until she came to my church to hear me preach. I had reached out to some friends and said, "Hey, I don't get to do this every week, but this Sunday I'm preaching in 'big church' and I'd love for you all to come." I was a youth pastor at the time so preaching to the congregation was a special opportunity for me.

She, along with a group of our mutual friends, came to support me. While she sat watching me preach she developed a crush on me. Why? I made her laugh. She thought my jokes were funny. It sparked an interest, and now, here we are married with three kids!

When you make someone laugh it causes them to trust you and builds a stronger bond between you according to an article in *Psychology Today*:

> "Anybody can make you cry, but only certain people can make you laugh. Laughter releases endorphins, which make us feel good about ourselves and others. This good feeling creates a bond between two people and imbues a sense of togetherness in groups. The Golden Rule of friendship states that if you make people feel good about themselves, they will like you—and laughter does just that. It makes you feel good about yourself and the person who triggered your laughter."[7]

When you make your listeners laugh while you're preaching, it can make them like you simply because

---

[7] People Will Like You if You Make Them Laugh by Jack Schafer Ph.D. (https://www.psychologytoday.com/us/blog/let-their-words-do-the-talking/201608/people-will-you-if-you-make-them-laugh)

laughter produces that result. Why should you want your listeners to like you? Likability and trust work together to form a powerful tool: *influence*. John Maxwell's leadership coaching can be summed up in one phrase: *Leadership is influence*. The ability to make your audience laugh is just another way to gain influence as you build trust with them.

Humor brings people back into paying attention. Have you ever been reading a book only to realize that you don't know what you just read? Even though you were looking at the words on the page, reading them and turning to the next page, your mind was somewhere else. Your listeners do the same thing. They may be in the room, sitting in the seat, facing toward you, but that does not mean you have their attention. Their minds could be going a million different directions.

This is where humor can be so powerful. You can use humor to bring those people back into paying attention to what you're saying. Don't believe me? Have you ever been in a setting where everyone started laughing at the same thing, but you missed it? You perk up, you ask the person next to you, "What just happened? What's so funny?" People do not like missing out on laughter. The same is true for your listeners. Humor is a way to capture and keep their attention for a moment so you can lead into your next thought with them fully engaged. If you can make everyone laugh, you can win back the room.

I hope you can see at this point that using humor has a host of benefits for you as a preacher. But you may be asking how do I use humor? You may wonder if humor is for you, especially if you consider yourself to be lacking in the funniness department. In the next chapter we'll look into how anyone can learn what it takes to be funny and use humor when they speak.

CHAPTER NINE

More Than Joke-Telling
How to Use Humor in Your Sermons

When I was a youth pastor I occasionally hosted an event for our middle and high school students where we would turn the youth room into a coffee house complete with café tables and chairs, a pleasing ambiance, fresh brewed coffee and espresso, and a stage open for live music and other displays of talent.

I was always blown away by the giftedness of our students. Some sang, others played instruments, and others did spoken word or comedy sketches. In most cases it was pretty incredible to watch how skilled these kids were at performing.

But at one of these events a student in our group, we'll call him Jeremy, wanted to try his hand at stand-up comedy. He told me he had a routine and was ready to go. When it came time for his slot our emcee introduced him, "Please welcome Jeremy to the stage. He's going to make us laugh with some stand-up comedy."

Jeremy proceeded to take the microphone, pull up the barstool and sit down. Everyone in the room, curious as to what he was going to do to make them laugh, gave him their full and undivided attention. You could hear a pin drop as people glued their eyes to him waiting for him to speak.

He froze for a few seconds then began to mumble through some barely audible self-deprecating comments about his apparel. Then he paused for the laugh.

Crickets.

Not getting the response he wanted he doubled down.

"That was a joke, it's okay to laugh!"

The crickets turn to moans and groans as people resumed their conversations knowing he wasn't going to deliver on the promise of side-splitting humor.

He kept trying for a few minutes, but it was evident that he clearly had no idea where he was going to take us. He was on stage to make us laugh, but he fell flat.

To the empathetic types, in case you are feeling badly for him and wondering if he lived through this, he did indeed survive and was able to laugh about his embarrassing comedy attempt later!

But his experience brings something to the fore that you may not realize if you've never tried it: *intentionally getting people to laugh can be tricky*. Especially if making people laugh is your *sole* purpose for being in front of a crowd. This is the case with stand-up comedy. It's way easier to fail than to succeed.

In fact, the main objection people have to attempting humor in their sermons is the fear of failing. Who wants the awkwardness of trying to be funny and having it fall flat? All of us have experienced the cringe-factor of a public speaker who attempted humor only to have the joke go up in the flames of unfunny disapproval. No one wants to put himself through this, and the good news is, you don't have to!

This chapter will demystify how to use humor in your sermons. I think you'll find that with a bit of practice, and a few tools, you'll be well on your way to using humor frequently and effectively. And you can avoid the fate of Jeremy!

In the same way that some people are naturally athletic while others (like me) have to work hard to be decent at sports. Some people are naturally funny while others have to work at it. While I believe wit and humor are natural inclinations of some people and not so natural to others, they are skills that anyone can develop with a little bit of study and hard work.

When you look closely at what makes people laugh you will see some patterns emerge – patterns that you will be able to employ in your preaching with a little practice.

A LESSON IN COMEDY: PREMISE, SET-UP, PUNCH

First, it's important to understand what makes people laugh: *the element of surprise.* When you're expecting one outcome, and another happens, it has the possibility of being funny. Spoiler-alert: Once you know this it will ruin stand-up comedy for you because you'll know what tactics comics are using to make something funny. Comedians start with a premise (a situation, a setting, a scenario).

Once they have described the premise, they will build the set-up. Both the premise and the set-up are designed to make you come to an obvious conclusion. Once you've done this in your mind, they will deliver the punch.

The punch is designed to divert away from the obvious conclusion you've made in your mind and shift to something counter to that. That surprise – the punch – is what makes you laugh if it's delivered the right way.

This may sound confusing, but it's actually quite simple. Let me give you an example. I heard a comedian recently say: "I would never put my mother in a nursing home! That just seems so … expensive."[8]

If we break this down, his premise is the dilemma of whether or not to put his mother in a nursing home. The audience is probably thinking about their own mothers or just mothers in general. They're thinking about how important it is to care for aging parents. They're agreeing in principle with him that it may not be the best decision to shove your mom into a nursing home. (Disclaimer: I'm just explaining his premise and what it is intended to do to the audience. I'm not saying I agree with it. There are fine facilities that take wonderful care of the elderly!)

After the premise comes the set-up. His set-up is in one line, "That just seems so…" The set-up is intended to get you to draw a conclusion about where the sentence should land. Given his premise – that he's not sure of the morals of putting his mother in a nursing home – you may draw the conclusion that he's going to say, "That just seems so heartless." Or "That just seems so uncaring." But remember, for it to be funny we need the element of surprise. The surprise comes at the punch.

His punch is simply one word: *expensive*. This interrupts where the audience thought he was going. So let's combine all the elements. As the listener, you're presented

---

[8] This line was delivered by Andrew Stanley in a comedy routine you can find by searching his name on YouTube.

with a premise that makes you empathize with an aging mother. You actually feel proud of the speaker because he is taking the high ground and sacrificing his own comfort to care for his mom.

Then, you're given the set-up that leads you to draw the conclusion that the speaker would never be calloused or uncaring. Finally, it's all wrapped up with a punch that interrupts the premise and flies in the face of the conclusion you have drawn. All of this together causes people to laugh.

An important practice to remember is to always put the punch at the end and particularly the last word you say. Then pause and let it sit for a second. It's not as funny when you keep adding phrases. For example, this is not as funny: "I could never put my mother in a nursing home! That just seems so expensive to do that to her." By adding the phrase "to do that to her" it walks all over the punch and makes it less ... punchy. The word "expensive" in this scenario hits your audience hard, and they need a second to laugh about it. When you keep talking it's called walking on your laughs, which is a comedy no-no.

Now, with this knowledge you can make anything funny. It's important to know that I'm not suggesting comedy hour where you stand and deliver a bunch of one-liners. That's not your job and your audience will tire of it.

But here's the cool thing: If you learn just this one principle, you can make your audience laugh in a variety of ways that can serve to illustrate your points, gain back attention, lighten the room, and do all the other amazing things using humor accomplishes. I want to explore two of them: funny stories and self-deprecating humor.

FUNNY STORIES

As we've seen in the chapter on storytelling, few tools are more effective than telling a story. But what makes a good story even better is when you can sprinkle humor throughout. This can work especially well when you tell stories about your kids or family life or friends. Using the premise–set-up–punch method above you can think through the parts of your story where humor could be inserted. Consider where you could lead your audience to a conclusion with a premise and set-up and then surprise them with a punch.

For example, I have a story I tell about going out for basketball in the 7th grade. We practiced for two weeks before it came time for them to separate us into A team and B team. I set it up to get my audience to think that I'm either going to be on one of those two teams. Once I am not put on the A team, I am surprised (and I let my audience experience that surprise) when I discover they made a C team and I was going to be on it! But not only that, I didn't even start on the C team. I was the worst basketball player ever to have gone through Mustang Middle School. That story is funny on its own, but it gets even more laughs when it is peppered with set-ups and punches.

When I tell the story I have certain places where I insert set-ups and punches that I have planned out ahead of time. When I deliver those they often get laughs because they follow the formula, and I have tested them with different audiences over time to know they are funny. The beauty of using humor in a story is that if a set-up and punch falls flat you just roll with it and move on with the story. Nothing is lost even if your attempt at humor falls flat. You'll kill it with some jokes and bomb with others. That's the nature of using humor when you speak.

SELF-DEPRECATING HUMOR

One of the best tools you have as a preacher is self-deprecating humor. Or, put another way, relatable embarrassment. You are a vast subject of humor and when it's you saying it your audience is less likely to take offense. This can get awkward though if you take it too far.

When I first started out in ministry I really wanted to relate to the outcasts and fringe kids in our youth group. I would tell stories about not being one of the "cool kids" in middle school. I embellished a bit for comedy's sake. Some of the students started to feel really bad for me. Others couldn't relate because of how outlandish I made my uncoolness seem. I had to learn to be self-deprecating in an honest, relatable way.

You have to strike the right balance for you. Determine what is the right amount of self-deprecating humor that lets people see that you don't take yourself too seriously, but not so much that you cannot be taken seriously. It's a fine line, but in my opinion, the trustworthiness and humanity that you build with your audience is worth it.

PITFALLS TO AVOID WHEN USING HUMOR

Humor can be an amazing tool for all the above reasons, but it also has the potential to shut people down and close them up. In the same way that humor, generally speaking, causes your listeners to trust you and like you, the wrong kind of humor can have the exact opposite effect. Here are some pitfalls to avoid when using humor in your sermons.

Humor that doesn't fit your audience. Communication is not about the speaker; it's about the listener. It's about God's using your words to help spur life-change in them. This means that you need to know your listeners well enough to gauge how they would respond to a particular attempt at humor. You may have something hilarious you want to say, but will they get it? Does it fit into the culture of your church? Chances are, in most cases, the answer is yes. But you need to make sure you have a firm grasp on their lives and what they are going through so you can use humor that will land on them and not just leave them confused.

If you have an idea for something, but you think it's risky, run it by your preaching team (I go into detail about why you should have a preaching team and how to form one in my book *Preaching Killer Sermons*). Ultimately, you have to decide when to push and when not to.

Shock-jocking. Shock jocks are the guys on radio and podcasts who use coarse language and vulgarity to "shock" their listeners and boost ratings. It works for a lot of radio personalities. Sometimes preachers will try the same tactic. They will use sensitive topics as an opportunity to use crass language and coarse humor.

Depending on your listeners, you risk alienating people who may be offended and decide not to listen to you. My suggestion is to avoid being offensive for the purpose of shocking people. If you teach the Scriptures it will be offensive enough on its own. Tell the truth and use humor to relieve the tension, but don't seek to capitalize on the opportunity for a moment of attention-getting.

Overdoing the same jokes. If you preach in the same church long enough your listeners will get to know everything about you. They will become intimately acquainted with your stories, your experiences, your preferences, and your pet peeves. They will also know your go-to jokes. Don't risk boring your audience by overdoing the same jokes again and again. One way to avoid telling the same jokes as well as the same stories is to have a robust preaching team that can give you feedback and keep you from falling into the same routines week after week.

Canned humor and cheesy jokes (unless it fits you). Don't take advantage of the fact that it's a church and people are more forgiving with what they'll laugh at. You should not use that as an opportunity to get lazy and tell corny jokes and use canned humor. It's a lazy approach and especially ineffective with Millennials as they cannot stand things that seem phony. I issue this one caveat: If cheesy jokes fit your personality, then you could embrace the cheesiness and use them how you want. Just be careful and don't overdo it.

I'm the king of dad jokes. Dad jokes are jokes that have obvious puns and moan-inducing cheesy punchlines. They're meant to be annoying and silly. They are a weak form of humor because they require little thought and leave people feeling like their intelligence has been insulted. They're called "dad jokes" because their sole purpose is to provide dads with an easy way to embarrass their kids. All that to say, I love dad jokes! I use them all the time, but if I were to use a dad joke while preaching I would say that's what I'm doing. I would do it ironically, which makes up for the cheesiness.

With those cautions laid out, I do want to say this. Humor is supposed to be fun, so more than anything, don't stress about it too much. If you are causing people to smile for a moment, you are winning with humor. Keep it up and have a good time.

PART THREE

MASTER THE EXECUTION

CHAPTER TEN

The Moment Matters
Bringing Your Listeners into an Experience

It was the summer after my sophomore year of high school. I was attending a leadership camp at a Christian university in Oklahoma. The first night of the camp I sat in the chapel of the university along with 1,000 other high school students for the evening worship service. Churches from all over the state had sent their student leaders to become better leaders in their student ministries and schools.

The evening worship session was much like a typical youth camp. There was music that was cooler and better than what we were used to back at our home churches.

There were some camp director types who got up and gave some information and rules for the week. But by far the highlight of my experience that night and for the rest of the week was the speaker. At that time, I had no idea who he was or what kind of an impact he was going to make on my life. I was ready, in that moment, for just another camp message.

But what happened was decidedly different. The speaker stepped onto the stage and owned the room. I don't know how else to say it. It was as if he walked into the atmosphere, grabbed it, and pulled us in with him. Every eyeball in the room was locked on him from start to finish. Toward the beginning of his message he said, "No more playing church, this week we are going to get gut-level real." I can still hear those words and feel the excitement I had about going on that journey. *I want to get gut-level real*, I thought to myself. It's scary and real and raw. Yes, I want that!

What did he do that was so special? He created a moment and ushered us into it. He set the expectation and invited us into an experience that was going to be worthwhile. This was a moment that no one in the room wanted to miss. We all wanted to hear more. That speaker was Craig Groeschel, and he's still one of the best communicators alive today.

It has been said that people may not remember what you said, but they will remember how you made them feel.[9] On the journey toward mastering preaching we must understand and fully utilize the power of creating moments in which we help our listeners feel deeply. It is in emotions and feelings that people are motivated to make change. Emotions create tension, and when people are in tension they move. Tension causes action. Tension must be broken through and resolved. When you usher people into a moment of tension, they have the greatest chance of responding with life-changing action.

CREATING A MOMENT

What is the secret to creating a moment? Fortunately there is no "secret" to it. Rather, there are principles and practices that you can learn and develop so that it will become more natural to create compelling moments for your listeners. I want to show you three ways you can create moments in your sermons and use those moments for tension-building and life-change.

You will find that opportunities to create moments are often embedded in what you are already doing when you preach. The moment you want to create exists inside your message when you tell a story, make a point, or give an illustration (to name but a few examples).

---

[9] This quote has been attributed to multiple sources going back decades according to https://quoteinvestigator.com/2014/04/06/they-feel/

When you tell a story. We've seen at this point in our journey that stories are an effective tool to utilize in our messages. A story is also a great place to create a moment. I realized this recently when I was rehearsing a message at our staff meeting where we pre-record the upcoming weekend message. (Here's a bit of an aside but worth mentioning: We always pre-record the sermons as a contingency in case there is a glitch in one of our campuses that receives the sermon on video. If we need to switch from the live video feed to the pre-recorded one we can do so seamlessly. I highly recommend this if you do video teaching as a multisite church.)

In the sermon I was pre-recording I told a story of how my wife and I had miscarried our first pregnancy. The pregnancy went ten weeks, we had seen the ultrasound, and we were having twins. It was a devastating blow to find out we had miscarried our babies. We worked through it, grieved and healed, but it was tough. But as I was telling the story in this sermon several years later I did not attach the original emotion to it. I did not dig deep into the memory of how I felt when it happened. I did not feel it, I just said it.

As a result, the staff who were hearing the message didn't feel much about it either. When we were evaluating the message as a part of our get-the-sermon-ready-for-Sunday process, the feedback I received about the story was that it could have been more powerful. They said I could have brought them into that moment of pain and made them feel what I felt. Then I could have asked them to look inward to the type of pain that they have felt.

Fortunately this was a pre-record, which in our context is just a contingency. This is the benefit of rehearsing in front of a group of people because I was able to dig deep into that memory and figure out how I would tell that story differently so that I could take my listeners on a journey with me and actually bring them into a moment.

It turns out on Sunday, I got more comments about that story than anything else in my message. The point of the story was not just to make people feel sad and shed a tear or two. Rather, it was intended to get them to consider the age-old question of why God allows certain things to happen to us when they are painful and cause us grief. By bringing them into a moment and making them feel real emotions that question moved from an academic exercise to real life. It was no longer a theoretical consideration about a theology of pain. Rather, it was a true-to-life scenario of grief, sorrow, and what we are supposed to do with it.

How did I bring them into the moment with that story? How can you bring your listeners into the moment with the stories you tell? The key is to be authentic and not try to force it. People know when you are trying to manipulate them. And if the story is true to your life you won't have to manipulate a feeling. It will be real, and that will show.

In addition to authenticity, I had to slow down and walk through the moments in time when the story unfolded. From our expectation and excitement that we were pregnant for the first time, to the laughter-inducing but joyful realization that we were having twins, to the fear and uncertainty of one of them having a slow heartbeat, to the expectation that at least one would pull through, to the overwhelming sense of loss and grief when we realized that two of our little loved unborn babies no longer had beating hearts. Even writing these words brings back the emotions of those moments.

All I did to invite people into a moment with this story was to recount those points in our journey and be transparent about how they affected my wife and me. I explained what I was thinking in those moments whether my thoughts were full of faith or marred with doubt.

Rather than trying to force a moment to happen in your next sermon, consider a story you are already telling and ask this question: How can I bring people along in this story so that they feel what I felt, think what I thought, experience what I experienced, and see what I saw? If you can do that you can create a memorable moment when you tell a story.

When you make a point. Another way you can create a moment is simply when you make a point. Much like my story example above, I realized this when I was preparing a sermon about Heaven. One of my points was that Heaven was going to be a place where 'we will be free of sorrow, grief and pain.' Once again, my greatest feedback came from my rehearsal time during pre-record. I presented this point with matter-of-factness. I showed the scripture, said the point, reiterated with more scripture, and moved on. This is not what I teach and I knew it was inadequate, but I wasn't sure how to break through. A piece of feedback I received helped me know what I needed to adjust in my presentation. They said, "I want to experience the joy of being free of sorrow, grief, and pain. Make me feel it."

I had merely *stated* a fact. I had not made it visceral. Consequently, I had not created a moment. With that feedback, I was able to correct course when I preached that message on Sunday. I asked everyone to think of one of the worst times in their lives. This is admittedly not a fun exercise but important to the moment. I asked them to remember back to that moment of pain. To let it sink in. Then I said, "Now I want you to consider that in Heaven, there's none of that." That one simple juxtaposition of the pain we experience on Earth with the sudden realization that in Heaven there exists none of that pain is enough to create a small moment for people. It is far more impacting than stating a fact devoid of any real life emotion.

You can see that change was subtle. It was not much different from what I had originally done to make that point. But that subtle, simple change went a long way to help people enter that moment and have a stronger connection to the reality of Heaven and what we have to look forward to in eternity. A point is just words until it makes sense in real life. By allowing people to feel the point you make, you help make the Scriptures come alive in people and help them see God's Word more clearly.

The next time you make a point, think through how you can make that point come alive and allow your listeners to feel the truth of it. One great way to achieve this is to draw a contrast as I did in my example above. Another method you could try is to acknowledge the counterintuitive nature of the point. A lot of what we teach seems counterintuitive because the gospel is counterintuitive. God becomes one of us and dies for us in our place? That doesn't make sense, but it's beautiful. Many points we make are ways of communicating bits and pieces of the gospel. Where they don't seem to make sense on the surface, acknowledge it and allow your listeners to put on their skeptic hat for a moment.

The key is to not try to overdo it but to look for opportunities to make your point land on people in such a way that they have to deal with it, whether they agree or disagree, in that moment and wrestle with the truth presented.

When you give an illustration. In the same vein as creating a moment when you make a point is to do so when you give an illustration. You can create small opportunities for people to enter a moment with you and fully connect to the truth you are illustrating. A simple example of this from my sermon on Heaven was when I was trying to illustrate the beauty and magnitude of Heaven. I talked about driving through the Smokey Mountains for the first time.

I could have just said, "I drove through the mountains and they were huge and beautiful. Heaven is even better!" That statement is true, but nobody would feel like they had been with me in those mountains. Instead, to create more of a moment, I said, "Being from Oklahoma, I was so used to flat land that the first time I drove through the Smokies I was blown away. I'm in a 4,500 pound SUV and yet I felt so small compared to the enormity of the boulders and cliffs that were to my left. I looked to my right and realized that if I made one wrong move I would tumble down the side of the mountain. It was exhilarating. I realized in that moment how small I am compared to God's creation. Think of a time when you were blown away by the realization of how big and expansive the world is. As amazing as those experiences are, Heaven is even more magnificent."

Once again the change here is subtle, but the key is to figure out how you can give people the opportunity to go on a journey with you experiencing the illustration, or story, or point you're making so that they feel the gravity of the truth it is communicating. The simplest way to do this in any of the three areas is to simply walk through every feeling, experience, fear, emotion, and excitement that you have attached to it and walk your listeners through them, inviting them to experience all of it along with you.

SHIFTING FROM MOMENT TO MOVEMENT

There is an end-goal to creating a moment, and it is *not* to get people to nod their heads and say, "Mmm, that was deep." The end-goal of creating a moment is to allow people to experience the tension required to change. The goal is for your listeners to apply the truths of Scripture you are communicating and live them out. In other words, we want to shift our listeners from the excitement of the moment to rubber-hitting-the-road movement.

The key is to communicate so that the truth should result in action. A lot of your listeners may have a tendency to think a particular principle is great for someone else to apply. Your role is to get your listeners to see themselves applying the truth and taking the next step in their spiritual journey.

Seeing themselves applying the truth. There is a lot of power in visualization. If you can paint a picture for your listeners of a potential future it can be very intriguing to them. In *Communicating for a Change*, Andy Stanley details the sequencing method he uses for every piece of communication he delivers. I would recommend reading more about it in his book, but his five-step sequence is "Me, We, God, You, We," and in these five steps the communicator shows how an idea relates to them personally (Me), broadens out the examples so that everyone in the room can relate, which builds tension that everyone can feel (We), teaches through the Scriptures to reveal the truth that applies to the tension (God), gives specific application points so that everyone listening knows how the truth is lived out practically (You), and concludes by casting the vision for what it would look like if everyone listening applied the truth collectively (We).

There is so much brilliance in that sequencing because it can be applied to any piece of communication you can imagine. If applied correctly, this sequence can be an effective tool for creating a moment. My favorite part of the "Me, We, God, You, We" sequence for shifting your listeners from that moment to movement in their lives is the "You" section. In this part you offer practical, real-life ways people can and should apply the truth if they want it to work in their lives. Even if you don't use Stanley's five-part sequence, you can still communicate the "You" section effectively.

The key is to think through your content holistically and consider how to give as many real-life examples of how it applies as possible. The beauty of this approach is that you can apply it throughout the entire sermon. You don't have to wait until the "You" section to give examples of how the message could be applied. Instead, in the introduction build tension by giving examples that touch on as many different types of situations as possible (Me, We) Then, in every point and during the "You" section, apply the message to more examples. In this way it will not come across as a list but as a natural flow from point to application to illustration and back.

How do you give examples? Use your preaching team during your preparation to think of how your message will land on as many different people as possible. In your message, describe people's situations to them as if you completely understand where they're coming from and what they're going through. Here are some examples:

- You're here today and you're wrecked with guilt from what you did last night. You think God is mad at you.
- You've never made a habit of giving, and you're hesitant to get started. What if today were the day you decided to trust God in this way?
- You're married, but you have someone at work whom you find yourself attracted to more and more. You haven't crossed the physical barrier, but emotionally you are connected. Give that to God today and make yourself accountable to a friend before you go to work tomorrow.

When giving examples it does not matter that they don't apply to everyone. They don't have to. They will likely apply to someone, and if they're varied enough, they'll hit close to home with others even if they don't describe their exact situation. The point of giving examples is to get people to think about their lives and see themselves applying the truth to their lives.

Taking their next step. It doesn't stop there because people love "seeing" themselves do something and "considering" what it would be like. But, to shift people to movement, you have to get them to take their next step. I'm a firm believer that everyone at every point has a next step to take – from the most seasoned veteran who's been following Jesus for decades, to the person who's just checking things out but still skeptical. How do you get people to consider their next step and take it? It's important to acknowledge that you can't make people do anything – nor would you want to. Your job is to present the truth in a compelling way and let the Holy Spirit do the life-changing. But there are two simple things you can do to help put people in the position where they are listening to the Holy Spirit's guidance and taking that next step: Ask questions and extend challenges.

First, ask questions because application does not always have to be a "to-do." Sometimes application can be a "to think" because as I stated earlier, the Holy Spirit is going to work in your listeners' lives as they wrestle with how a truth fits into their experience. A question is sometimes the prompter to get them to look inward and pay attention to what they're thinking and feeling in that moment. In other words, your sermon may be the catalyst to get someone to question the way they've been living, their worldview, or their daily practice of walking with God. Asking a question is a great way to get your listeners to do some introspection – to look inside themselves and see what they find.

For example, if you preach a sermon on obedience to God's Word your question could be, "What's one thing in your life that is keeping you from obeying God?" Or "What step do you need to take today to begin walking in obedience?"

Second, extend challenges because some sermons more naturally call for a specific challenge. You have different listeners with different personalities. Some people like to be lovingly called out and challenged. Some people are saying, "Hey, step on my toes! It's what I need in order to take action!" When I'm preparing I ask myself what challenge I could extend in the sermon. If it flows naturally, I'll do it.

Say you preach on the importance of giving regularly. Your challenge could be, "Give something. Start today. Try it for three months and see how God is faithful to you."

A moment can be a catalyst in the life of your listeners. Practice the art of creating moments and work on shifting people from the awe of the moment to the life-changing action of movement.

CHAPTER ELEVEN

Smooth Delivery
Eliminate Distractions, Be Ready for Anything

My wife and I have three daughters. At the time of this writing they are ages four, two and one. So we have fairly recently experienced three baby deliveries.

In each case I was amazed by the doctors and nursing staff at the hospital. It was as if they considered beforehand every possible distraction and hiccup that could occur. They had plans and contingencies in place to deal with just about anything.

We were incredibly fortunate this was the case in two out of the three deliveries because there were minor complications that came up upon delivery that could have turned tragic in a hurry.

But they knew exactly what to do and began executing according to their training immediately. This, in one case, saved the life of my wife, and in another case, saved the life of my middle daughter as they both had unforeseen complications that occurred that needed immediate and skilled attention.

Had the doctors and nurses not been prepared and had not planned ahead for such complications it could have been a tragically different story.

When it comes to preaching, a smooth delivery is vital. If we are properly prepared, we can handle anything that comes up and ensure that all the preparation that went into writing the sermon is not wasted on sloppy delivery.

As we seek to maximize our impact as preachers we must be cognizant of certain obstacles that can negatively affect our ability to smoothly deliver our sermons. We want to eliminate any distraction that pulls our listeners' thoughts and attention away from the content of the message and onto something else.

This is why I want to walk you through two major potentially distraction-causing obstacles to watch out for in your sermons: *distracting physical habits and last-minute changes*. Identifying and eliminating distracting physical habits and mastering best practices for when you change some or all of your sermon content at the last minute will serve to catalyze your preaching impact.

DISTRACTING PHYSICAL HABITS OF PREACHERS

Every preacher has physical tendencies that unintentionally distract the audience. Sometimes the preacher is aware of these while other times they are tics and habits that must be pointed out to be changed. Public speaking in any context, including in a church setting, engages your whole mind and body. This means speakers can easily find themselves neglecting to pay attention to their body language and physical habits because they have to remember what to say ... and everyone is watching.

All of us could use some coaching in this area. This is why watching your game film is so important. I watch the video of every sermon I preach. This helps me see what others see when I preach and has proven invaluable to me as it helps me know what to improve.

I want to offer five common physical distractions I've observed in preachers over the years. I've also seen a good amount of these in my own preaching over the years and have sought to correct and eliminate them.

Turning your back to the audience to read from the screen. I love when a preacher decides to ditch the notes (more on that in chapter thirteen). However, one unintended consequence of such a departure from the traditional notes-on-the-podium model is that preachers go from staring down at a page, to turning their backs to the audience and reading from a screen behind them. This is a common rule of any stage presentation: Never turn your back to the audience. Turning your back to your listeners is weird and awkward, except in the rare case when you are making a point that the back-turning illustrates. For the purposes of reading from the screen, don't turn your back to your audience and stare up at the screen and read from it. The audience does not want to see the back of your head. A great alternative is to use a TV-on-a-stick right next to you on stage. This way you can point to it as you are speaking and not draw your attention away from your audience.

Using filler words and vocal pauses. If you want to dramatically improve the delivery of your sermons overnight, do this one thing: eliminate filler words and vocal pauses from your sermon delivery. What are filler words and vocal pauses? I cover this more extensively in chapter ten of *Preaching Killer Sermons*, but in short we use these words when we fill in the gaps of our speech with throw-away words like "um" "uh" "you know" "like" and others. They are a huge distraction because they don't allow people the opportunity to soak in what you've said. Instead, they fill the silence with what essentially becomes noise to your listeners and causes them to tune you out entirely.

Don't believe me? Try this next time you preach: Find a good place in your sermon to go completely silent for three seconds. Maybe after you make a point, or read a verse. Whatever the place in the sermon, pause for just three seconds without warning. Don't fill the silence and don't explain what you're doing. Here's what you'll notice: Everyone will look up. They will momentarily attend to what you're saying. For that instance, you have them. What you say next is vitally important because all eyes and ears are on you.

But if instead of pausing, you were to say "Um, uh, uh" and then give your next thought, you would have far fewer people paying attention in that moment. Give it a try and experiment with it. It will motivate you to do what it takes to stop using those words.

Aimlessly pacing back and forth on the stage. In college I majored in Communications. In this program, we studied presentation techniques extensively. We examined what works and what doesn't when it comes to public speaking. And we practiced presenting in front of each other routinely. In the first speech I gave as a freshman in this program, I paced a lot, back and forth across the room. I was mimicking what I had seen some of my favorite speakers do. The difference was, their pacing was purposeful and intentional while mine was aimless. My professor called me out on it and said, "Stop it with the pacing! It adds nothing to your speech."

When I observe preachers' stage movements, I can often determine whether they've thought through their motions and how they come across onstage. The problem with aimless pacing, especially from one side of the stage to the other, is it wears your listeners out. Not only do they have to pay attention to your content (what you are actually saying), but subconsciously they are also trying to make sense of your movements (what you are doing). If your pacing and movements are incongruent with what you're saying, your listeners will notice this and get frustrated with you and stop paying attention.

You do not want to risk this. But how do you know what pacing is okay? Should you ditch it altogether and just stand still? Couldn't pacing be helpful if it is intentional? I would not recommend ditching movement altogether. It can be another tool in your public speaking arsenal if it is intentional and purposeful. When it comes to stage movement, however, keep a few best-practices in mind.

First, remaining relatively still is better than aimless pacing, so if you are going to err do it on the side of standing in one spot on the stage. Second, if you do decide to try stage movement make your movements congruent with your content. When you shift to a new thought, use that transition to move on stage to support or bolster the transition to the new idea. This could be as simple as turning and walking a few steps parallel to your audience. Your body movement signals to your listeners nonverbally that a new thought is coming.

Finally, your gestures and hand movements should align with the vibe of what you're saying. If you're making a big, powerful point then a big powerful gesture is appropriate. Perhaps in this case you could open your arms wide as if to embrace the power of the truth you're communicating. Similarly, if you are communicating something contemplative and introspective you should bring your gestures in tighter to your body as if to convey a sense of intimacy and thoughtfulness.

I adapted those three best practices from watching Craig Groeschel sermons and hearing him discuss the purpose behind his stage movements. For a great example of how to do stage movements in a way that is purposeful and intentional, check out any of his sermons on his church's website at life.church. You can also learn more about his rationale and thought behind how he does stage movements in an article I wrote called "The Communication Secrets of Craig Groeschel" which you can find on PreachingDonkey.com.

Constantly adjusting the head-worn microphone or clothing. A lot could be said about microphone usage while preaching. Head-worn mics are increasingly common as the cost of the technology has decreased. A head-worn mic usually consists of a small wire that holds its shape around one of your ears and has a small extension that comes down your cheek just beside your mouth. The actual microphone is on the end of that extension. These mics are designed to be relatively unseen and you don't have to hold them. The cord goes down your back, best when under your shirt so it is hidden, into a receiver pack that makes the wireless feature work.

I see pastors constantly adjusting the cord that goes down their back because their clothing pulls on it. So you'll see the speaker grab at the cord from just below his ear and pull up. The cord will work its way back down and he'll pull it up again. This becomes habitual to the preacher and a major distraction for the audience.

There's an easy fix: Clip the cord to the back of your collar. A lot of Countryman mic kits come with a clip for this purpose, but they get lost or just go unused. If I can't find the clip I grab a paper clip and connect it that way. No one can see it and it holds it in place.

Another related distracting habit is the tendency to adjust clothing. Pulling down the shirt, pushing up your sleeves, or (the absolute worst) adjusting the crotch area of your pants... awkward! Avoid these tics by rehearsing in exactly what you intend to wear when you preach. This will allow you to determine if the ensemble is going to work onstage.

Not fully articulating words or finishing your sentences. If you've ever had to speak on camera and had a good videographer coaching you, you know how important articulation is on camera. Ways of expressing yourself that seem over the top in regular conversation come across as normal on camera. This is why you may be coached to smile bigger, speak louder, articulate clearer, and gesture wider. In the moment it seems ridiculous, but any videographer knows that if you don't express yourself in that way, it will result in a dull video.

It is much the same when preaching or public speaking. If you have a tendency to mumble or not finish your words or sentences, it has astronomical effects on how your listeners perceive your speech. Perhaps they can't understand what you said because you didn't articulate your words clearly. Or they can't fully hear you because you are speaking too quietly and without passion.

In any case, the failure to articulate is a huge distraction. Practice saying what you're going to say and make sure each word could stand on its own. Make sure each sentence, each thought, makes sense and could stand on its own as a complete thought. This is an effective way to overcome this common habit. It will feel forced at first as you get used to speaking with more pronounced diction and greater clarity, but you'll be a better speaker and a better communicator if you stick with it.

So there you have it. Those are some common physical distractions to work on. When pursuing smooth delivery, also pay attention to what can happen when we change the plan at the last minute.

LAST-MINUTE CHANGES

I recently preached a sermon where I felt God was leading me to change up the introduction entirely. This occurred to me minutes before I was about to preach. I sat on the front row during worship and it was clear to me that the plan I had for the sermon opening just didn't fit. The direction I felt like God wanted me to go was to share a personal story of my dealings with sexual temptation as a teenager and into college. This was a risky proposition when completely extemporaneous, but I've told the story many times so I went with it.

This experience made me think about the best ways to ditch your plan when you feel like God is leading in a different direction with the sermon. Here are six pointers to keep in mind:

Prepare well. The better prepared you are the easier it is to deviate from the plan. You won't be wondering how the sermon wraps itself up if you've prepared well enough to know. So much rests on preparation, but if you are going to change something up last minute you should definitely make certain that you are prepared for such a departure from what you had prepared. Can you pull it off? Will you be able to look over the passage and solidify your thoughts with enough time to make adjustments?

Don't make a habit of it. Your listeners will begin to question your sincerity if you default to ditching the plan too often. They'll wonder if you ever even have a plan.

Not to mention, the people running your media elements (slides, videos, etc.) will grow weary of your ever-changing plan.

Avoid announcing your change of plans to the church. This happened as a near constant in the churches I grew up in. The pastor would get up and say, "Well, I had a message prepared today, but I feel God is leading me to speak on something entirely different. So instead of Romans, turn to 1 Kings." This kind of warning can make people expect the sermon to be bad because it is off-the-cuff. If they're expecting it to be bad it probably will be in their minds. Sometimes it's unavoidable to mention it if you've provided message notes and your sermon is different. But to the extent you can avoid bringing attention to it, I would.

The same principle applies if you get up and say, "Well, I didn't have a lot of time to prepare this week so 'bear with me' through this." Let me speak for your congregation: "No! We don't want to bear with you! All you've said is that for the next 30-40 minutes you're going to waste our time with whatever jumbled mess you manage to stumble through." Sound harsh? It's meant to. The only thing worse than not preparing well to speak to God's people is telling them you're not prepared.

One half of your listeners will respond how I've described above. The other more empathic half will respond by feeling badly for you while cringing through what they hope is not an embarrassing and awkward experience for you. Needless to say, you don't want either of these reactions. You set the tone for how people feel when they're listening to you. Avoid giving them reasons to be distracted with unhelpful (and unnecessary) thoughts.

Only preach an entirely different sermon in rare instances. First of all, I'm not saying God can't or doesn't lead in this way, but all things being equal, I don't recommend preaching an entirely different message from the one you've prepared except in rare cases. If a tragedy recently struck your town or a child in the church suffered a life-threatening injury, it would be fitting. When there is something catastrophic it makes sense to drop the plan and walk your congregation through it. But, generally speaking, you should avoid changing up the plan entirely if at all possible.

If you notice that you're doing this with some regularity, you should consider how tuned in to God's leading you are in your preparation. I fully believe that God speaks to us in our preparation and not just in the moment.

If you know in advance, let the right people know. Let your worship leader know, the people who advance your slides, and anyone involved in follow-up or post-sermon prayer. Make sure the right people have warning if you can give it to them.

Preach as if it is what you prepared all along. If you change up only parts of your sermon, leaving the main points as planned, you will likely be the only one who knows. No one knows what's on your personal preaching notes but you anyway. So, if you change up the plan, your audience may not even notice unless you tell them.

Pray. I only recommend changing up the plan if you really feel God is leading in a different direction. You must be in prayer during this process to know exactly where you should take the sermon.

LANE SEBRING

CHAPTER TWELVE

What Are You Talking About?
Avoiding the Curse of Knowledge

I moved from Oklahoma City, OK, to the Washington, DC, area straight out of college at 22 years old. It was an adventure to say the least. DC is a fast-paced, high-capacity, leader-saturated, type-A-personality-laden, beautifully diverse, traffic-jammed, long-commute-every-day, action-packed, never-a-dull-moment place to live. I loved it. The people there blew my mind by how intrinsically driven they were to succeed and change the world in the way they felt it needed changing.

It was exhilarating but, at the same time, intimidating. I was a kid from the Midwest who had not seen much of the world (or even the U.S. at that point). I quickly discovered there was a lot I didn't know. It wasn't my fault I didn't know these things. I just didn't know what I didn't know.

So I found myself constantly in situations where I would meet someone and we would do the usual, "What do you do?" exchange of pleasantries. I would tell them I was a youth pastor, which was my job at the time. They would then tell me what they did for a living. In almost every case for the first few months I would have no idea what they were talking about. They would give me their title or describe what they did, but neither would make any sense to me. They would say they were a contractor. I would think construction. But they were not talking construction, they were a defense contractor for the Federal Government. I was just supposed to know that. Or they were some complicated type of engineer or developer or lobbyist or worked for a think tank. Think tank? Is that like a dunk tank?

I quickly realized that, in most cases, these roles and positions were common knowledge to *everyone* but me. It was as if they all got together and learned this stuff and I was left out. I would nod my head and say something like, "Oh, cool, that's great." But inside I would be thinking, *I hope they can't tell I have no idea what they just said.*

I lived in DC for ten years and eventually became one of those people who understands all that stuff. But at first, those conversations left me feeling ignorant and somewhat isolated.

THE LAST THING YOU WANT TO DO

There are people in your church every week who have a fraction of the knowledge you have about who God is, what Jesus did, what the Bible is and how to read it, what "sanctification" means, what "salvation" is referring to, and so on. When you talk about your "quiet time" they wonder who got in trouble and was apparently sent to time out.

This is a fact you should wrestle with: The ideas and concepts that are so common knowledge to you that they seem mundane would blow someone else's mind. But the problem is that many preachers don't take time to explain complex concepts because they think, "Everyone knows this." Or worse, "Everyone *should* know this." As a result they limit their ability to speak to certain people because they speak over their heads.

Why does it matter that you understand this reality? Every time you preach you run the risk of making people feel isolated and even stupid just because they don't know what you're talking about. This is the last thing you want to do when you preach. When people feel stupid they become insecure. When they're insecure they close up and wall off to protect themselves. When they close up and wall off they are not open and willing to hear your message. You. Do. Not. Want. This.

And, not to mention, they probably won't come back to your church.

THE CURSE OF KNOWLEDGE

What I'm referring to is the Curse of Knowledge. According to Wikipedia, it is defined this way:

> "The curse of knowledge is a cognitive bias that occurs when an individual, communicating with other individuals, unknowingly assumes that the others have the background to understand. For example, in a classroom setting, teachers have difficulty teaching novices because they cannot put themselves in the position of the student."[10]

If you are a seminary-trained pastor with vast experience teaching and preaching as I am, you are at prime risk for the curse of knowledge. In fact, even without formal seminary training, you are a high risk for the curse of knowledge if you preach with some regularity, read theological books, and study the Bible.

Think about it. The curse of knowledge happens when we unknowingly assume that others have the background to understand. Pastors do this all the time. So if

---

[10] This definition is taken from Wikipedia: https://en.wikipedia.org/wiki/Curse_of_knowledge

it's something we are unaware of, we have to train ourselves to be aware of it. This will help us to stop assuming, because you know what we do when we assume...

LET'S GET REAL ABOUT WHY WE DO THIS

In addition to unknowingly assuming that people know what we know, I think we pastors are inherently motivated to sound confusing because of three mindsets that get tend to drive us. I would bet you can relate to one or all of these.

You would be embarrassed if someone thought you didn't know a truth or concept. There may be theological truths and biblical concepts so common knowledge to you that you can't fathom someone not knowing them. You think, They should know this! Doesn't everyone know this? Consequently, you wouldn't want to run the risk of making people think you don't know it or that it is new to you. And you certainly would not want someone to think you're still wowed by it.

So you end up blazing through ideas that seem simple to you to get to the more complex matters. In this case, you are more concerned with how you look than with communicating clearly with your audience. What's tragic about this is that your listeners take their cues from you about how they should feel about a given topic. If you seem unmoved by something because it's "old hat" to you, they may never experience the wonder you first experienced.

You preach to an imaginary audience of biblical scholars. Pastors have a tendency to preach to impress their former seminary professors who don't even go to their church. Or they want to impress the new family who recently started attending because "they just weren't being fed" at their last church. Pastors feel this pressure to perform for those people and "feed" them so they get nice and fat. So they ignore the needs of the spiritually young to satisfy the needs of people who are going to eventually find fault with them anyway before moving on to the next feeding station.

I once heard the following story and it made a huge impact on me. A young pastor, fresh out of seminary, was preaching way over the heads of his congregation. Motivated to be deep, theologically rich, and biblically sound he sought to preach faithfully. And he meant well. There are certainly worse things to be concerned about. But he was not connecting. A mentor counseled him and said, "You have all these great teachers, mentors, church fathers, and theologians behind you. All this training you bring to the table. That's good! But your back is to your church because you are so concerned with impressing your mentors. Turn around, face your audience, and with all that knowledge in your arsenal, speak to your people."

A lot of preachers need to metaphorically turn around and preach to those who are in front of them. They are your flock. Focus on feeding them, not by trying to impress your mentors by turning your back to your church.

Now, for the people with arms crossed in your audience saying, "We already know this stuff. I just want to be fed. This isn't deep enough." Translation, "I want to leave confused by what you said so I don't have to do anything with it, but I can pat myself on the back for attending a theologically rich church. Go me!" Don't be concerned about impressing those people.

It's a constantly moving target and you won't hit it most of the time. Instead, view it as an opportunity to come alongside such people and teach them to have compassion for unbelievers and those new in their faith who don't know everything they know.

HOW TO AVOID THE CURSE OF KNOWLEDGE

Finally, here a few action steps to put into motion to overcome this curse of knowledge. I think these practices will be helpful for you in this challenging, but worthwhile, process of learning to speak in a way that your audience understands and connects.

Gain the heart of a teacher first and foremost. A teacher doesn't loathe her students for not knowing something before she teaches it. She revels in the joy of revealing new concepts to them. As a preacher charged with feeding our sheep we should be all the more eager to take painstaking care to deliver concepts in such a way that people can ingest, digest, and use for spiritual fuel.

As we've seen, preachers have a lot to overcome to be able to communicate clearly to people who do not have the same training they have (virtually everyone in your church). So it is vitally important that we approach every sermon with the desire to do everything we can to make the gospel clear and the Scriptures come alive in the hearts and minds of our listeners. This step has much more to do with where you heart is than what you are actually doing. Are you looking to impress scholars or impact lives when you preach?

Understand that you have people in your audience who are in all spiritual conditions. There is nothing more maddening to me than when I hear a preacher say something like, "Well, we're all believers in this room." How do you know? You don't know! And by saying something like that it reveals to your audience that you're speaking to and for the people who already identify as believers. If you are going to overcome the trap of the curse of knowledge, you must do the work it takes to understand your audience and know the spiritual condition of as many people as you can.

If you are going to assume something, assume this: You have people in *all* spiritual conditions in your audience. People struggling with addiction, affairs, pride, loneliness, doubts, fear, and abuse. You also have people who are walking closely with Jesus and living Spirit-filled lives. Your preaching must appeal to all of them to take their next step.

Ask yourself: "Would my unbelieving friend know what I mean by this?" This is a helpful method. Think of people in your life who have little or no knowledge of scripture and ask yourself if they would understand. If they wouldn't, how would you explain it to them? If you're not sure they would understand, try asking them. That might start a good conversation.

If you can't think of one unbelieving friend, get out more. That alone might be a sign that you need to engage more with "regular" folks and learn to speak their language a bit more.

There are certainly more ways to overcome the curse of knowledge, but I find these three steps the simplest way to get started and the best way to remind myself continually that I need to have the heart of a teacher, to understand that I am speaking to people in all spiritual conditions, and to speak in such a way that people who know nothing about faith would have a clue what I'm talking about.

There is no way to avoid completely the effects of the curse of knowledge. Why? For the simple fact that there are always going to be people with below baseline understanding of basic biblical knowledge, which is going to be even more pronounced as the culture becomes less biblically literate. That said, you can do everything in your power to make sure that you are intentionally thinking through how to engage and connect at every level and leaving no one to feel ignorant and isolated, but inviting them to taste and see that the Lord is good.

BUT "EVERYONE" IN MY CHURCH IS ALREADY A CHRISTIAN

An objection that might arise depending on your context and situation sounds like this: "But, in my church, I know everyone and they're all believers. It would be unnecessary for me to explain theological words and concepts because they all already know them." In the same breath the pastor usually laments the church's lack of growth. They build a model on preaching to the proverbial choir and wonder why no one else is showing up in the pews. There are a couple considerations here that will be helpful if this is a hang-up for you.

First, it's simply not true. It is dangerous, and beyond your capacity, to determine the spiritual condition of everyone in your church. People can be great at faking it, and it's a lot to assume that you know when someone is and isn't legit. Be careful not to assume that just because you see someone at your church often and involved regularly it means he or she is walking with Jesus and tracking with everything you are saying.

Second, when you speak to who's not there, they show up. Responding to the question "How do I grow my church when it is small and has very few visitors?" Tim Keller said something that has always stuck with me: "Speak to who's not there and they will eventually show up."[11] He said the biggest reason for this is because when you tailor your message so that you are answering objections that you anticipate skeptics would have, and you put deep principles in words that a layperson can understand, and you make an effort to speak *to* unbelievers and not *about* unbelievers, it signals to your audience that it is a safe place to bring their unbelieving friends.

People are risking social capital when they invite their friends to church. You have to demonstrate, and prove over time, that you are not going to damage the equity they have with their friends. Does this mean you compromise the message? Not at all. What it means is that you assume unbelievers are there and you engage them in a way that's compelling and intriguing.

---

[11] I saw Tim Keller respond to this question at a conference for pastors and church leaders. He also builds out this principle in his book Preaching: Communicating Faith in an Age of Skepticism (2015) New York: Viking Press.

Beyond demonstrating to your folks that it's okay to invite people, preaching to who's not there does a lot of for you as a communicator as you are working to maximize your impact. It diversifies your reach as you become a multi-dimensional communicator who is equipped to understand and speak to a variety of life-situations and people. It increases your ability to put yourself in other people's shoes and empathize. All of these put together make you a more compelling communicator to a broader audience.

It's important to keep a few best-practices in mind when making an effort to speak to those who are not currently in your church but *you want them to be*. First, don't speak *about* them, speak *to* them. If you've ever been in a room and had someone speak about you as if you are not even there you know how awkward that can be. "I'm right here!" is the response most people give when placed in that situation. Don't do that to your listeners. Speak to them by engaging them, giving them a voice, and making them feel understood and heard.

Second, avoid using "Us and Them" or "We and You" language. Avoid anything that has a ring of "You're not part of us" attached to it. Be sure to utilize your preaching team by asking them to help you speak to more kinds of people every time you preach.

CHAPTER THIRTEEN

Maximize Engagement
Ditch the Notes, Own the Room

We've all seen this happen. The preacher walks up to the stage with a Bible, some pieces of paper, and a binder. He spends the first few seconds placing everything on the podium. While he's doing this the audience is mostly looking at the top of his head as he looks down. As he begins speaking he reads from one piece of paper, looks up, finds another one in his binder, reads it, looks up again, and then looks down for his next idea. Aside from the sloppiness and the seemingly unprepared vibe this gives off, it also risks not engaging the audience.

Let's contrast that scenario with the preacher who gets up on stage and speaks with clarity and command of the room, engages everyone with eye contact and energy, and you never see him look down, fumble through pages, or read from anything but the Bible.

From a communications perspective, the preacher in our first scenario is far less likely to connect with his listeners. He is missing a vital aspect of grabbing people's attention immediately. In fact, the first 90 seconds of any message are the most important for gaining and keeping the audience's attention.

In *Preaching Killer Sermons*, I suggested three must-do practices for a strong sermon opening: Start high, start clear, and start now. Understanding these three must-dos will be important to you as you consider your usage of notes. *Starting high* just means that you should come out of the gate with energy and enthusiasm. This energy will be contagious to your listeners and signal to them that something worthwhile is about to happen.

Starting clear means that you very quickly clarify for your audience where the sermon is going and why it's worth it to pay close attention. In most cases this means you are building tension and creating interest, but it is clear to your audience that it is worth it for them to keep listening.

Finally, *starting now* simply means that you must realize there is no time to waste. You should not spend precious moments fumbling through notes, clearing your throat, adjusting your clothing, and not engaging your audience. To start now means that you engage your listeners with relevant and engaging content as quickly as you can.

Returning to our contrast of the two approaches: The first preacher could neither start high, start clear, nor start now. Instead, he was so distracted with the assembly of his preaching set-up that he could not deliver energy, clarity, or urgency.

The preacher in our second scenario is freed up to bring passion, clarity, and urgency to his message right out of the gate. He will not only grab his listeners' attention more quickly but has a much more likely chance of maintaining the audience's attention throughout the sermon.

This is all because he isn't fumbling through notes. Instead, he's free of notes and freed up to engage with his audience and deliver.

Recently, I began to be intrigued with this idea: What if I could train myself to not need notes at all? What if I could prepare in such a way that I could deliver a message and never look down but maintain eye contact and physical engagement with my listeners from start to finish? What if you could to?

So I began training myself not to use notes, and I want to share with you how to preach without notes. But first, I need to address one objection you may have right now.

SOME CAN HANDLE NOTES WELL

Wait! you might be thinking. *The preacher in the first scenario is bad with notes, but I'm good with notes!* What I can say is, so am I. I'm really good with notes. They're on one page, in my Bible, and I rarely look at them.

I want to make it clear that I don't think notes are bad. In fact, a lot of preachers use notes extensively and do it well. Sam Storms at Bridgeway Church in Oklahoma City is a great example of someone who uses an entire manuscript when he preaches and does it excellently and engagingly.

My notes were already much more minimal than a full manuscript. And, as I stated above, I was good at navigating them smoothly. But I began to experiment with ways to not use my notes at all. Because, regardless of how well I handled my notes, I still found myself depending on them, which meant diverting attention away from my audience and onto something that only I could see. This will be important later, because I am not suggesting not reading anything at all, but I am suggesting not reading anything your audience cannot also see.

THE SKINNY ON PREACHING WITHOUT NOTES

So even if you would consider yourself effective at using notes, what if you could train yourself to go one step further and not use them at all? What if you could have just as much of a content-rich experience without ever diverting attention away from your listeners?

I want to share a simple four-step process that will enable you to ditch your notes entirely. This may take longer for some than others, but if you work this process you will be free of your dependency on notes altogether.

Step One: Reduce the amount of notes you allow yourself. I would not suggest getting up this Sunday without notes if you are currently accustomed to using them. This may lead to forgetting your message entirely, causing panic to wrack your brain. Instead, begin reducing the amount of notes you use. If you currently use 3 pages, see if you can get everything onto 2 pages. Maybe after getting used to 2 pages, you can reduce your notes to 1 page. Eventually, you get used to what you have, so reduce it a little at a time and keep moving down until you get to 1 page.

This exercise is important because it teaches you to drill down on what the most important ideas are. As you eliminate pages of notes you end up distilling the most important things to communicate, which end up being the bones of your message. I have found the easiest way for me to do this is to build my message notes around triggers and key ideas.

Step Two: Build a flow of touch points and triggers. Think through your message in terms of a flow. In the simplest terms, your message will begin with some sort of introduction, which will flow to the body of your content, which will flow to a conclusion. All along the way you can set up triggers that will help you think through what is next in your sermon. On my one page of notes that I still write for every sermon I have a system of touch points and triggers. Even though I rarely read from them on stage, it is still helpful to make the notes as it helps me internalize my message and be able to deliver it without using my notes.

To build this out in your notes ask two questions: What are my touch points? By this I'm not just talking about main points but also every illustration, example, story or thought you want to communicate along the way. The second question is: How can I use triggers to tie them together in my brain? This second question is essential because if you're going to ditch the notes, you have to drill down a logical flow that makes sense to you.

If you're looking at your one page of notes, you should see a flow of touch points (ideas you want to communicate) and triggers (things that tie them together). This will enable you to see, at a glance, how the entire message flows. This is the same method some actors use to memorize lines. They break every scene down and know that first this happens, then I say this line, then she walks across the room, then the door opens and I say that line, etc. I'm not suggesting you approach a sermon like an actor saying lines. But, in much the same way, the method of building logical flow in your message will help you move away from dependency on your notes.

Step Three: Rehearse and internalize your message. The next step is to take that one page with your touch points and triggers and rehearse. I make the argument for rehearsing, out loud, every message you deliver. You can read more about rehearsing in chapter five to see why it's so important and how to do it effectively.

But for our purposes, you can't preach without notes if the message is not in you. The way the message gets in you is by internalizing it. This is different from memorizing it. Memorization is what you do when you cram for a test. Internalization is when the touch points of the sermon, the important ideas you want to communicate, are burned into your heart and mind. This allows you to let what is inside of you come out rather than just trying to memorize what you wrote down.

When you lose track or forget, the triggers come in handy. They help you remember your flow and stay on point. This all comes from internalizing, which happens most effectively when you rehearse. This leads to the fourth and final step.

Step Four: Use presentation slides to your advantage. Remember earlier I said that you want to avoid diverting your attention to something that your audience can't also see? Here's what I mean by that. If I have a piece of paper on stage with me and I look down to read it, I'm looking away from my audience and onto something else. This provides an opportunity for my audience to disengage with me and my content.

But what if I could bring my audience's attention to a scripture or key idea that we read together? What I'm referring to is the screen, which is nothing new. But I want to give some suggestions on how to make the most out of it. First, consider using a TV on stage with you. I have used a TV on stage with me for years after seeing Andy Stanley pioneer this idea several years ago. What this allows me to do is draw my listeners' attention to the idea as we read it together. Because it is a TV right next to me they don't have to divert attention away from me to see it. In certain cases, depending on the size of the room, some will be watching on the big screens, but they'll still see the same thing: me engaging a scripture, idea, or concept with them.

This method allows me to still read ideas and concepts onstage but do it with the audience coming along for the ride. But that's not the best part. We have confidence monitors in our auditorium. A confidence monitor is just a fancy way of describing a screen that is pointed at the stage instead of at the audience. When I'm preaching only I can see the monitor. Using ProPresenter software, I can see my current slide and my next slide. So all I have to do if I get stuck is look up at the monitor and see what the next slide is before advancing to it. This serves as a trigger for that next touch point as I generally have each slide represent a major touch point I want to communicate. The beauty of this is that the confidence monitors are placed in such a way that when I look at them it just looks like I'm looking at the audience.

Those four steps are how I have been able to move away from notes and to a more engaging delivery. Give it a try. The key is to stay persistent until you are able to free yourself from notes altogether. Just remember it takes time and you don't need to rush it. Move along at a pace you're comfortable with and you'll become more natural at not using notes as you go along.

LANE SEBRING

CONCLUSION

The One Thing You Can't Do Without

My hat is off to you! Few people make it all the way through any book, so great work! I want you to consider what you've accomplished at this point on your way to becoming a preaching ninja.

You have identified and dealt with the destructive mindsets that could negatively affect your preaching. You walked through the crucial first steps of pursuing preaching and preparing sermons. You have developed systems to rehearse and evaluate your messages. You have worked on becoming a better storyteller and using humor effectively to capture your audience when you preach.

You've discovered how to bring your listeners into the moment and keep them there. You've finally ditched the notes for a more engaging approach to delivering your sermons. You have learned to avoid the pesky, but common, curse of knowledge that plagues most preachers. And finally, you've discovered the importance of preaching to who is not there and have found that they seem to show up when you do that!

In a word, you've developed. You have grown and honed your craft. You are on a course to maximize your preaching impact, and I am thrilled that I had the chance to be a part of this with you! But there's one more thing…

THE ONE THING YOU CAN'T DO WITHOUT

I probably shouldn't tell you this, but everything you've discovered and put into practice does not mean anything without one incredibly important element. In fact, you could do everything I've written about in this book and it will still fall short if this one thing is not present in your preaching. What is it? The Holy Spirit's power.

You know this. I'm confident you know this truth intellectually and that you could stand up and give a powerful sermon on it right now! But knowing a truth and living a truth are two different practices altogether. Let me encourage you with this challenge: Make reliance on the Holy Spirit's power in your preaching a top priority and practice for you.

Something supernatural takes place when you stand up to preach. I'm sure this has happened to you at one point or another. I've experienced this in my preaching a number of times. Before the sermon begins, I'll feel a sense of inadequacy, insecurity, or doubt about myself, my message, the people's receptiveness to it, or all the above.

Then I walk out on the platform to preach and something changes in me. In that moment I am relieved of those feelings and doubts and, instead, filled with a sense of confidence, or as I like to call it, "Godfidence" in what God can and will do through my message to impact lives and point people to Jesus.

HOW TO RELY ON THE HOLY SPIRIT

This happens largely because every sermon, especially the ones I enter filled with self-doubt, are prime opportunities for me to build trust and reliance on the Holy Spirit's power to work through me and in me during the message. How does this happen? How can this happen for you? There is no formula, but there are steps you can take toward a deeper reliance on the Holy Spirit during your messages.

Pray and ask God to work through you. The first step to ensuring that your preaching is filled with and fueled by the Holy Spirit's power is simple: pray. Though it seems obvious, we often overlook this step in the shadow of writing and preparing our sermons and developing ourselves as preachers. What a tragedy it would be to be diligent to prepare the sermon without preparing your heart to preach it! You will not experience Holy Spirit-led preaching if you are not in tune with the Holy Spirit.

I make a practice of praying before, during, and after my sermon prep process. Every step of the way I'm asking for guidance, wisdom, and God's power to work through me. Continual prayer is vital to your ability to preach effective, Holy Spirit-led sermons. Trying to preach without prayer is like trying to drive a car with no oil in the engine. You may be able to make the car go for a while, but without the oil it will eventually burn up.

Do everything you can do to prepare well. As I've run a website and hosted a podcast on preaching and now published two books on preaching, I've come across this recurring, yet flawed, sentiment among some preachers: *The more I prepare and work on delivering my sermon, the less I am relying on the Holy Spirit to lead me in the moment.*

The tendency among these preachers is to neglect rigorous preparation in favor of a more spiritualized reliance on God. This is a false dichotomy. The Holy Spirit can and does lead and guide during your preparation on Tuesday as much as he does on Sunday.

You should not substitute one for the other. Rather, seek to have God's guidance both during your prep and delivery. How does this happen? The Scriptures instruct us to study to show ourselves approved. That means we are commanded to prepare our sermons diligently and give it all we have and leave the rest up to God.

Make a practice of confession and repentance. To preach in the Holy Spirit's power you must walk in the Holy Spirit's power. As preachers, it is imperative that we continually remain surrendered to the will of God and follow his lead daily in our lives. Part of this practice is going to mean we regularly confess and repent of any known sins we have.

Apart from this regular repentance and submission to God's will we will experience powerless preaching. Many preachers can get away with this for a while – some longer than others – but eventually an un-surrendered preacher will find himself preaching unremarkable, ineffective sermons.

It has been said that you can't give what you don't have, and that is especially true in preaching. Keep short accounts and make sure sin is not affecting the joy of your salvation.

Check your mindset. We began this journey by examining the mindsets that we are prone to adopt that are counterproductive to our preaching. Our preaching mindset is the story we tell ourselves about our preaching.

To remain reliant on the Holy Spirit I encourage you to examine your mindset and make sure it is a healthy one.

Do what the Scriptures teach and take your thoughts captive (2 Corinthians 10:5). When destructive thoughts creep in, reject them and replace them with a better story. The better story is that God can use you. God wants to use you. God will use you. As Paul says, choose to take whatever is true, noble, excellent, praiseworthy, or admirable and think on those things (Philippians 4:8).

Lean into your calling. When doubts come in and invade your heart and mind, the one reality you can lean into and find reassurance is in your calling. In a previous chapter, I discussed how to confirm your calling. Once you know you're called to preach and there is no denying that calling, it is a confirmation that can carry you through a lot of challenges and setbacks. A calling comes from God, so knowing and leaning into your calling is a way of leaning into the Holy Spirit himself.

I want to leave you with words from the Apostle Paul when he was instructing a young pastor, Timothy, on how to lead and pastor people faithfully. Reflecting on his own journey, Paul said: "I thank Christ Jesus our Lord, who has given me strength, that he considered me trustworthy, appointing me to his service" (1 Timothy 2:12 NIV).

Lean into the reality that God considered you trustworthy enough to give you the task of speaking for him.

Work to be worthy of that trust by doing all you can to maximize your impact, but learn to lean on God's strength and leave the rest up to him. He is the one who changes lives. You get to be a small part of it when you preach. I get to be a small part of it when I preach. May we revel in that reality, and keep preaching on!

LANE SEBRING

- Main idea (key idea that will hold together) → in the title
- Why should someone listen? recurring theme. reword.
- Will it be relevant?
- Hook → a good question... / funny story / illustration
  - you need to answer question.
  - What you will get out of it.

- Body - tension/points - where are you getting that?
  - see Ken's work
  - have can't, have can, have come.
  - teach - illustrate - apply

standing out
How do we stand out in HS / college?
- Grumbling?
  How don't grumble?
  to each other do for?

- Do gods want to grow?

- Application - challenge w/ the reasons from the body
  → has to be bold.
  → spirituality very important as preacher.

cast a vision - "could you imagine"

Storytelling → clear purpose - details - talked about...
  connection to context - wit - structure / the end in mind.
  relevant details - time limit - what's your point
  clear / compelling / interesting. - tension, issue,
  protect people's identities drama.
  - 3 P's
  feels / funny / fail

Humor → likeable - feel good - guard down
  laugh - w/ someone
  pyramid   trust - draws you in / interested
  setup   relieves tension.
  punchline. element of surprise

ABOUT THE AUTHOR

Lane Sebring is a pastor and the author of *Preaching Killer Sermons*. He is the creator of PreachingDonkey.com, a site dedicated to helping preachers communicate better. His articles have been featured by SermonCentral.com, Church Leaders.com, and Pastors.com. Lane has a B.A. in Communication and a Master of Arts in Pastoral Ministry. He lives in Knoxville, TN with his wife, Rachel, and their three daughters.

LEAVE A REVIEW ON AMAZON?

If you benefited from this book, please consider leaving an honest review on Amazon! Reviews help more pastors see the book and benefit from it. It's easy to leave a review. Go to this book's listing on Amazon and you'll see where you can leave a review. Your words are much appreciated!

BECOME A PREACHING NINJA

Made in the USA
San Bernardino, CA
06 February 2019